SMALL
STORiES

BiG
TEAM

D1713045

Small Stories - Big Teams:
Everyday stories that build extraordinary teams.
By Derrick D. Sier

Copyright © 2017 by Derrick D. Sier.

Published by Derrick Sier & OMOS Team Building.
PO BOX 721395 Oklahoma City, Oklahoma 73172
405.412.0473

International Standard Book Number: 978-1544051727

Printed in the United States of America

Cover design and formatting by
Kristen McGregor - Astrea Design.

Edited by Chatoya Duarte –
CF Creative Communications.

SMALL STORIES

<< EVERYDAY STORIES THAT BUILD EXTRAORDINARY TEAMS >>

BiG TEAM

DERRiCK SiER

T A B L E of C O N T E N T S

ACKNOWLEDGMENTS >>

This book is the result of several story lines of my life coming together to create the perfect mix of me. If I tried to tell them all, this project would be exhaustively long. Additionally, there are just as many people who have played their part within those stories and if I tried to list them all, I wouldn't do the list justice. From my parents to past employers to professors to friends to classmates, there is no way I could list and expound on all the ways each of you have individually impacted my life. However, there are a few people who have gone above and beyond to make it a personal goal of theirs to usher me toward success. Late night phone calls. Impromptu meetings. Showing up early. Leaving late. Sitting through a thousand of my questions. These people have personally invested in my success and are definitely worth mentioning.

In summer 2004, I walked into the University of Central Oklahoma without much direction. I knew I wanted to work with people. I knew I enjoyed recreation. I knew I had a growing interest in social and group dynamics. But I didn't know how any of those interests could combine. I worked in the wellness center as a field supervisor and intramural official. I was a part of the degree club. I built relationships with classmates and professors, hoping to find some fields of interest or professional direction, but continued to strike out.

It wasn't until my senior year that things began to take shape, which was greatly influenced by Jerel Cowan. Jerel is a professor who started his teaching career as I began to complete my undergraduate career. For some reason, we gravitated toward each other immediately and connected very easily. The more I reached out to him, the more he poured into me. To him, I was more than a student. And to him, life was more than books and concepts. He made the content come alive and he showed me how to make it real for others. It is that platform from which I jump every single day.

In 2005, I walked into an event at a coffee shop and observed a guy talking to every single person in the room. He remembered names, made eye contact, laughed genuinely and interacted individually and personably. Eventually, he made his way around to me and we've been talking since. He has showed me the value of relationships and pursuing my passion. He has emphasized the importance of community and leadership. He showed me the impact and value of putting others first. He has dragged me into every single business venture he has launched and makes sure I stay ahead of the curve. He serves as coach, mentor, example and friend. He has opened his home, wallet and heart to me without fail or filter. I love his heart for people and his heart towards me. This guy is Gregory Coleman. I love you, Heady. #GoWin

Last, but not least. I would not be where I am today, without my wife. A million thanks to her for working a full-time job while pregnant so I could finish school and then supporting me through a second degree. A million kisses for raising two children and keeping a home while I chased my dreams. A million hugs for allowing me to run back and forth across the country, without hindrance, trying to build something great. To the woman who makes all the soccer games, all of the basketball games, every performance, rehearsal and practice, each doctor's appointment, yet manages to scratch my back, rub my head until I fall asleep and keep all of the nay-sayers at bay. To say the least, I love you Tequia Sier. You are my pea.

And to everyone else who has invested in OMOS,

sowed into my life and opened their ears and doors to my big ideas—thank you. For every hug, high five, chest bump, handshake and animal noise. Thank you.

To Heather Strong, Stephen Sheffield, Bracey and Lakisha Dangerfield for being my safe place. To Steve Ely, Mark Hollingsworth, Robin Wood, Jeannie McMahan for mentoring me back to health. To Kary Ott and Landon Dean for being true believers in my work and encouraging me without fail. To Clay Skoch, my vice-president. To Sarah Gaines, for truth and honesty. To Vintage Coffee for being my home away from home. To Arjaybi's Concepts for handling OMOS with care. To Danielle Hoeltzel, my sounding block. To Mom for being my biggest fan. To Dad for my work ethic, social nature and teaching me to care for people.

It is out of the depths of our relationships that I write this book.

DEDICATION >>

TO MY TEN SQUAD,
THE GREATEST
TEAMMATES I
WILL EVER KNOW.

FORWARD >>

While writing this book, I noticed that many of my thoughts naturally gravitated toward the business setting. This wasn't initially my intent, as I see the placement of group and social dynamics in every facet of life. While writing this book, I have been dealing mainly with organization conflict and creative solutions. So, I think those things just grabbed my attention. But the truth is, for the most of us, business is the smallest component of our lives. Sure, there are people who are…what they do, but for the most part, many of us are able to leave business at work. Because of that, I want to emphasize that regardless if you are at work or home, the fundamentals of relationship extend to every area of life. Good manners, ethics and morals, honesty, hard work, teamwork and selflessness has no borders. There are very few places on the planet that don't have people. Which means we all should desire to learn how to interact with them in a way that benefits both sides. We should always desire to grow relationally and to be a part of healthy functional teams. That is exactly what this book is about.

The old adage is true: there is no alphabetical "i" in team, but there are definitely individuals. This saying was created to emphasize the importance of unity, not to dismiss the existence and importance of the individual. In fact, that saying started to bother me so much, whenever someone said it, I would often reply, "But there is an M and a E." Because it's true. There is a ME. And there is a YOU. And every team is made of people just like us. And those people have stories. And those individual stories come together to make great stories. And great stories have the potential to impact the smallest of families and the largest of communities. And the MEs and the YOUs get to be a part of something larger and have an impact towards something greater than we could ever imagine when we realize our small stories are a part of a big team.

Whether at work or at home, I believe the concepts in this book will help. It'll help your church, athletic team, marriage, family, neighborhood and friendships. It'll provide hope for relationally bleak situations, spark life into dull moments and push you out of the mud and towards vibrant relationships in all aspects of your life. And it's not done by giving you direct answers. Every situation is different. It varies from person to person, group to group, environment to environment. But more so by creating a conversation within yourself through the reflection of questions and encouraging you to get better by completing the challenges at the end of each story.

Yes. These are my stories and my perspective. But put on my glasses, use your eyes and let's work towards a better you. Because if you get better, your team can't help but follow.

INTRODUCTION >>

When OMOS Team Building initially launched, the focus was on using experiential learning as an opportunity and avenue for others to discover the importance of teams. I passionately wanted people to see the value they bring to every team, no matter the setting, as well as the value of the person next to them. Whether that person is a co-worker, spouse, family member, neighbor, classmate or simply lives in the same city, they have value and it is vital that every member of that team understands that fact.

This passion arose from having been a part of several dysfunctional teams. These were teams that saw everyone as replaceable, irrelevant and discretionary. And in an effort to address those dysfunctions, I participated in several insufficient and ill-equipped team building sessions. During one, in particular, I specifically remember thinking how pointless it was because the content was not applicable, the scenarios were so far removed from our individual and collective experiences and when we got back to the office, nothing would change. In fact, it would probably be worse. Later, I found out that several other team members felt the same way, and unfortunately, things did get worse. This was the dying pulse of a group that had stellar potential. It happened all because we couldn't figure out how to operate as a team.

How does operating as a team look like? It is very important to understand that the perfect team is elusive— unattainable even. There will never be a team without conflict— never a team that always fires on all cylinders. However, there are teams who constantly pursue perfection. Those are the teams whose focus is on growing better together. Those teams pride themselves in their ability to weather the storm and come out stronger. They find every opportunity to bond so they can stand the tests of time. They stand up for each other, correct each other in love and respect, push and pull one another toward their fullest potential and fight to stay connected. Those are the pillars on which great teams are built. Those teams are fearlessly protective. They live in the moment, yet plan for the future. They hold every member closely and combat every threat. They are the team that may have stronger relationships amongst fewer people, but aim never to be exclusive. Those teams never proclaim perfection, but instead acknowledge their flaws and welcome the challenge to overcome them.

It hurts me to say we were not that team. We didn't even push to *become* that team. Those pillars of teamship weren't even on the radar. If you had asked us, we would have boldly proclaimed that we had transcended traditional work relationships and had become family. Truth be told: we were not even close to family and nowhere near a team. Looking back on that group, we should've looked inwards for solutions instead of outwards for help. Why? The solutions to our dysfunction were closer than we thought. The answers were in our hearts, our motives, our actions and our ethic. There were opportunities for us to grow better together every single day and we missed them. It is on those everyday opportunities which this project aims to land.

During this project, I worked to highlight moments that most teams miss daily, like paying attention to signs that their team has the potential to be great. I want everyone to notice how these opportunities are often overlooked, seen as too small to address or too insignificant to bother. In reality, those moments are the perfect opportunities for any team to shine and grow; to be nursed back to life through a daily dose of unity; to rid the group of a dying pulse and stimulate their potential to be great and sincerely grow better together.

This book is a collection of my thoughts gathered over several months. Many of the stories are completely unrelated, while several will be presented as a group of interrelated stories. In either case, this is the way I am inspired to see teams each day. I see teams in many different ways: playing with my son, volunteering at church, sitting in business meetings, watching television, hanging out with my wife and with my daughter. By the end, I hope you are inspired to view life through a similar lens.

As you make your way through this book, I encourage you to take time to consider the questions and complete the challenge at the end of every section. **The challenges are designed to provoke individual and collective changes and create a healthy culture over time, not provide an immediate and unavoidably temporary fix.** You can take one concept a day and finish it in a little over 10 weeks or cover one concept each week and finish it in a year. In whichever way you choose to complete the book, do it with care, open mindedness, sincerity and with personal and collective growth in mind.

This book should hit home on many different levels for you. You'll begin to see the various number of teams to which you belong, how they function and how you can make them better. Your heart will be pricked, conviction will follow and your morality, professionalism and ethical fiber will move you to action.

YOUR FIRST CHALLENGE

It is going to be easy to see others in these stories. Before you began to see others and point the finger at them, I challenge you to first see yourself. Confront your issues internally then publicly model the change you want to see in others around you. Your action and sincerity will be more effective than anything you could have said out of spite, frustration and not having first challenged yourself. If you **change yourself, your surroundings will follow.**

Change, too quickly, causes anxiety and resistance. Change, too slowly, breeds forgetfulness and exudes passivity. Change, appropriately, creates understanding, sustainability and ownership.

It is not until you've worked together that heaven is seen; until you've operated as one that the design of humanity is discovered; until you've found your place on a team that purpose is revealed.

There are five things that should be able to hold any group together. They aren't as grand as you may think, but they do serve as foundational ingredients of every successful group. I would even be willing to say that groups cannot reach their full potential without them, and should not desire to complete any task without at least three of these ingredients present at all times. These ingredients are not required, but serve as icing on the cake. And who eats cake without icing? Not this guy! (For the record, I don't eat glue, either.....anymore.)

The first ingredient is laughter. Humor is considered one of the top things desired most in a mate and/ or companion. It is no coincidence humor is also considered one of the most desirable traits of a co-worker. Think about it. A loyal and dedicated employee is often considered as being "married" to their job. Employee-employer contracts are signed. Co-workers are definitely known to flow in and out of a love-hate relationship. (They either hate the job and love the co-workers or vice-versa. Love-love is ideal; hate-hate is an explosion waiting to happen.) They share office space and must compromise quite a bit. They work together to accomplish goals, and often become familiar with each other's families. They might exchange phone numbers, with conversations covering a myriad of topics outside of work. The comparisons are remarkable.

Unfortunately, frequent interaction and personality differences bring tension. What better to make sure relationships continue to run smoothly than a good sense of humor? The ability to laugh at situations, yourself and each other continually lightens the mood and clears the air. People with a similar sense of humor tend to understand many other aspects of each other's personality. (I guess the same can be said about those with polar opposite senses of humor.)

Laughter is attractive. It releases positive endorphins. It relieves stress. And the light-hearted atmosphere of group work created by laughter is euphoric.

Of course, anything taken too far can be poisonous. Too much laughter and not enough of the other four components can lead toward the deterioration of a group. This is why laughter must remain in balance with the other components. Teams shouldn't laugh too little or too much.

What does this mean? Teams should laugh together. Teams should laugh with, at, for, around, and because of each other! Teams should produce funny stories and funny ideas together!

Laughter is one of the five ingredients of **group glue**. Groups that laugh, succeed and have fun along the way!

ASK YOURSELF

- What makes you laugh?
- What makes the people around you laugh?
- When was the last time your group has laughed together?
- Do you create opportunities for your group to laugh together on purpose?

CHALLENGE

Find a way to get your group laughing together regularly.

Laughter is attractive.

In part one of Group Glue, we discussed how laughter is one of the five ingredients needed to hold any group together. Very successful groups will most likely use these ingredients to concoct the glue that keeps them together. The second ingredient is **eating together**.

In many cultures, food is a social activity. It gives people something to do with their hands and mouths besides talking, and creates a more comfortable experience if talking isn't their thing. If you feel comfortable, you are more likely to show up and stay a while.

Food gives people something to talk about. Food draws people to a central location in which interaction will most likely occur. When there is food, people will come. If the food is free, people will flock. Plus, people just like to eat.

But *why* should there be an emphasis on eating together?

Because eating together gives the group a glimpse into part of your personality that may remained untapped in any other setting. You can learn a lot about someone through their table manners.

Do they wait for everyone to get their meal before they eat? If they are male, do they wait for the women to sit down first and stand up when they leave? Are their elbows on the table? Do they eat fast or slow? How do they take their water: with or without ice, lemon or lime, tap or sparkling? Do they wipe off their silverware? Do they share food or order dessert?

Eating, just like humor and the other three ingredients we'll discuss later, gives you access to a unique piece of a person that may not be accessible in other settings. Humor is going to show you something differently than the way someone eats. Ultimately, the glue of an individual contributes to the glue of the group. Eating together is one of the five ingredients of group glue. Groups that do it succeed and have fun along the way— and I'm sticking to it!

ASK YOURSELF

- How do meals work within your group?
- Who in your group prefers to eat alone versus with other people?
- Who eats in and who always goes out? Who eats at their desk, with the office door closed or open?
- How often does the entire group eat together? When was the last time? Should it be more frequent?

CHALLENGE

Sip some coffee with someone from your group in the morning. Invite someone else out for lunch. Meet up with someone else for happy hour after work. Repeat until you make it through your whole group.

You can learn a lot about someone through their table manners.

GROUP GLUE >>
PLAY TOGETHER (3 of 5)

In the first two parts of Group Glue, we discussed laughing and eating together as essential ingredients that hold a group intact. While they aren't as grand as you may think, every successful group most likely uses these ingredients to concoct the glue that keeps them together. The third ingredient is playing together.

There are certain rules to the playground: some are tacitly social, some are written and some are cultural. Whatever the case, no one can deny the fact that rules exist. For example, in Tag, no one chases the slow kid, right?! And if someone does, someone else eventually has to the let the slow kid tag them so the game can speed back up. Whether you like this rule or not, it's understood. No one talked about it beforehand. Everyone just understands. On the other hand, most groups will explain where you can touch people on the body if the group is coed. Correction. Especially if the group is coed. Those that abide by the rules get to play next time. Those that don't obey the rules either don't get to play next time or are shunned during the game. Whether the rules are obeyed or broken, spoken or unspoken, everyone must admit that guidelines are there and are important to the social and operational dynamics of the group.

To illustrate: Think about the person who plays aggressively during a laid-back game of basketball. Or the energetic newbie who enters a group of jaded veterans. I'm sure we've all experienced the guy who tells inappropriate jokes in a rather mild group setting.

Whether the playground is the office, church, the bar, the park, swimming pool, coffee shop, library, bike trail, or locker room, there are rules. How a person plays within the rules can let you know about other aspects of their character and personality.

Playing breaks down barriers; stress barriers, communication barriers, cultural barriers, social barriers, physical barriers, and emotional barriers. Playing energizes us, helps us meet new friends and find a place within the group. Playing takes us back to the simple days. And because the work environment tends to add pressure to life, what better way to cope and divert than to play. And it's just fun!

Playing together is one of the key ingredients of group glue. Groups that do it succeed and have fun along the way!

Listen—I'm sticking to it.

ASK YOURSELF

- What type of activities/games do you enjoy?
- What type of activities/games do the people around you enjoy?
- When was the last time your group has done something fun together, either work or non-work related?
- Do you set up opportunities for your group to have fun together on purpose?

CHALLENGE

Find a way to get your group having fun together regularly.

Playing breaks down barriers.

GROUP GLUE >>
DREAM TOGETHER (4 of 5)

So far, we've covered laughing together, eating together, and playing together — all of which are key ingredients that make up the glue that holds a group together. I know they aren't as grand as you may think, but every successful group will most likely use these ingredients to concoct the glue that keeps them together. The fourth ingredient is dreaming together.

I remember when I first shared my team-building dream in 2006. It was my graduating year of college. I used my senior project as a launch pad to create the OMOS team-building concept. Once it was developed, I let a few people see it before it was presented in class and given to my professor. While sharing it, I received a bit of generic encouragement and impartial interest, which was severely discouraging. Soon after, I crossed paths with a guy who shared and started a business based on those similar interests. We became close friends, worked together on several projects and he began to mentor me in this area. As a result of this relationship, the subsided fire that once fueled my dream began to rekindle. As the fire grew, my dream began to look like a possibility and that possibility would soon become a reality. I eventually founded and launched OMOS Team Building simply because my friend and I could dream together.

Dreams exist in the minds of everyone. Usually, these dreams remain in the mind as impossibilities. Sometimes, the dreamer gets brave and shares the dream, but more often than not, those dreams are received with generic encouragement and impartial interest. Then there's the unusual moment when someone shares a dream and the other person catches it. This power that comes from dreaming with dreamers is unexplainable.

Dreams are rooted deep within the soul. When people dream together, they are making a connection on a subsurface level that reaches a place untouched by laughing, eating and playing together. When more likeminded people plug into your dream, the process grows exponentially. You begin to see gains because your effort increases. Everything becomes a resource and because your perspective has changed, everything around you has the potential to fuel your dream.

This is why groups should dream together. Big dreams. Crazy dreams. Wild dreams. HUGE dreams. Scary dreams. Dreams that push, stretch, challenge and encourage the group as far as their imaginations will allow them to dream. Dreaming breaks up the monotony of traditional goal setting. Dreaming taps into the creative part of the brain that changes and challenges classical lines of thinking. Dreaming gives work purpose.

Yeah, I'm sticking to it. Dreaming together is one of the key ingredients of group glue. Groups that do it succeed and have fun along the way!

ASK YOURSELF

- What are your personal and professional dreams?
- Do you know the dreams of the people around you?
- How does your current job push you toward your dream?
- How do the people currently around you push you toward your dreams?

CHALLENGE

Find out how your current job and the people around you can help push you toward your personal dreams. Find out how you can contribute to your job's dreams/goals/aspirations.

GROUP GLUE >>
BUiLD TOGETHER (5 of 5)

Laughing together: Check. Eating together and playing together: Check and check. Dreaming together: Yup—check. Every one of them are essential and all are key ingredients that make up the glue that holds a group together. I know they aren't as grand as you may think, but every successful group will most likely use these ingredients to concoct the sticky stuff that keeps them together. The fifth and final ingredient, but not the least, is building together.

My son and I recently spent an hour building a medieval town complete with a moat, drawbridge, tunnel entrance, prison, guards, watch towers, wagons/carriages, horses, hippos, lions, monkeys, a bread shop....Robin Hood, and.... alligators. Did I mention we were using Legos? That's right. Legos. For an hour. My knees were so sore. My back was hurting. Who knew building a medieval town out of Legos for an hour would be so hard? And the weird thing about it — I would do it all over again in a heartbeat. Why? Because my son hasn't stopped talking about it.

People fear the building process. It requires work, effort and compromise. You have to tolerate and yield to others in order to build together. Ideas must be contributed, swapped and valued. Building together requires respect and cooperation. It also requires the ability to see the bigger picture, absorb the faults of others and share the success. There are ups and downs, as well as ins and outs. But in the end, when the group has built together what they could have never built alone, the end result will be worth it.

Yup, I'm sticking to it. Building together must be a key ingredient of group glue. Groups that do it succeed and have fun along the way.

ASK YOURSELF

- Who do you like working with the *most* in your group and why?
- Who do you like working with the *least* in your group and why?
- Who is someone in your group, with whom you currently don't interact with as much, but would like to interact with more? Why?
- How well does the group work together?

CHALLENGE

Find out what part everyone plays in reaching the group's weekly, monthly and yearly goals/projects. Look for ways in which everyone could work better together.

But in the end, when the group has built together what they could have never built alone, the end result will be worth it.

BUiLDiNG TOGETHER >>
BUiLD YOURSELF (1 of 5)

Now that we've discovered the secrets of group glue, it's time to start building together. Building is an important dynamic to group development. Individuals and groups, like companies, always must be in building mode. Think about it, people are the most valuable resource of any company. If the company desires to grow bigger and become better at what they do, they must first invest in the people who are doing the building. And **that** means companies must value their employees more that the systems in which they expect their employees to operate and more than the product they are trying to get their employees to deliver. Bottom line, if companies value their employees, the employees will make the sure the systems operate well and the product will be delivered with excellence. But what does that even look like? There are proven ways to build the product and operations of a company, but how do you build people? And how do those people work together to build groups?

The first look should be inward. *What can I do to build myself up?* You can independently pursue training and education. You can find a professional mentor or become a part of a professional organization. You can stay up-to-date on industry trends and become actively involved in the professional community inside and/or outside of work. On the most practical of levels, you can use your co-workers and job-provided professional development opportunities as resources.

It's fair to expect your job to contribute to your professional development, but that expectation must be preceded and fueled by an individual effort. Companies want to be reassured they are committing resources someone equally invested in bettering themselves. This concern can be easily erased by pursuing independent growth and taking advantage of every building opportunity provided by your employer.

Growth is your responsibility. People can shove it down your brain, but you must retain it. You can go to workshops, but you must listen and apply the information. You must open the book and read the content. It's up to you to take action. Build up yourself so you can be a strong and reliable resource to others.

Strong groups require strong individuals. Strong buildings require strong bricks. A strong bridge requires strong planks. Commit to building the best you that you can be. Once everyone decides to work on themselves individually, then you can build together.

ASK YOURSELF

- What are you doing to build yourself?
- Who holds you accountable?
- What areas in your life need the most attention right now?
- What kind of life do you hope to build?

CHALLENGE

Make a habit of building yourself physically, emotionally, professionally, spiritually, etc. Financially. Seek out professionals and experts for direction and instruction. The world is counting on you.

Companies want to be reassured they are committing resources to someone equally invested in bettering themselves.

BUiLDiNG TOGETHER >> BUiLD OTHERS (2 of 5)

The ability and desire to build is such an important dynamic to group development. Individuals and groups, like companies, always must be in building mode. But what exactly does that look like? There are proven ways to build the product and operations of a company, but how do you build people? And how do those people work together to build groups?

We've already identified **building yourself** as one of the ways to build something great together. The second way is by **building up each other**.

Spending time building yourself is necessary, but not to the point that you neglect everyone around you. The reason for building up yourself ultimately should be to contribute to something greater than yourself. This "something" can be your personal or professional community, family, friends, faith, etc., but something other than yourself.

This selflessness should be easy to spot within a group. Everyone should be eager to assist each other. Remember, the purpose of developing as a strong individual is so the group can be strong collectively. Most often, the group may look like strong individuals holding themselves up within their isolated responsibilities, but there will be times when its strength is shown according to how each person contributes.

I believe this to be the greater strength, as greater patience is required when dealing with others compared with ourselves. The same can be said with the commitment to communication, trust, forgiveness, time and many other variables needed when building the abilities and confidence of someone else in the group.

Strong groups require strong individuals. Strong buildings require strong bricks. A strong bridge requires strong planks. And sometimes, the strength of a building or bridge is directly related to how interdependent those bricks and planks are with each other. Remember, no single brick can operate as a building, and no single plank can operate as a bridge. We must remember to build together.

ASK YOURSELF

- When was the last time you helped someone do their job?
- Who in your group is easiest to assist and why? Who is the hardest to assist and why?
- How is your position unique within the group?
- What is something unique you, as an individual, bring to the group?

CHALLENGE

Find someone in your group whom you have never helped before. Find a way to assist them in completing a few of their tasks. Learn about them and their position with the group during the process.

Strong groups require strong individuals.

The ability and desire to build is an important dynamic to group development. Individuals and groups, like companies, always must be in building mode. But what does that look like? There are proven ways to build the product and operations of a company, but how do you build people? And how do those people work together to build groups? We've already identified **building yourself** and **building others** as two of the ways to build something great together. Another way is by **building relationships**.

Too often, people mistake frequency and proximity as relationship. Because we operate together frequently and in close quarters, we must have a healthy relationship, right? PUH-LEASE! I know couples who live with each other and don't have healthy relationships. And while proximity and frequency may **begin** a relationship, intentional acts are what create effective, resilient and meaningful relationships.

Strong groups require strong individuals. Strong buildings require strong bricks. A strong bridge requires strong planks. And sometimes, the strength of a building or bridge is directly related to how interdependent those bricks and planks are with each other. Remember, no single brick can operate as a building and no single plank can operate as a bridge. We must learn to build together.

ASK YOURSELF

- Who is the easiest person to talk to in your group? The most difficult?
- Are you easily approachable?
- What type of relationships do you desire at work, personally and professionally?
- How does being in a relationship with you bring value to others?

CHALLENGE

Take a long look at your relationships. Find at least three new ways in which you can bring value to others in your professional and personal relationships.

People mistake frequency and proximity as for relationship.

BUILDING TOGETHER >>
HABITS (4 of 4)

The ability and desire to build is such an important dynamic to group development. Individuals and groups, like companies, always must be in building mode. But what exactly does that look like? There are proven ways to build the product and operations of a company, but how do you build people? And how do those people work together to build groups? We've already identified **building yourself**, **building others** and **building relationships** as three of the ways to build something great together. The last way is by building good habits.

Building something great once doesn't make someone a builder. Instead, it's the ability to successfully repeat the process. In fact, not only successfully repeating the process, but also building better along the way.

What does building better look like? It's done by someone who is willing to learn from others around them, past process, failures and successes, and learning from people and groups who have found proven ways to build what they want to build. Once a better building method is discovered, building better must become a habit.

Strong groups and strong people have strong habits. They intentionally and habitually work to build up themselves, those around them and relationships between them. And like strong buildings are made of strong bricks and strong bridges are made of strong planks, strong groups must be made of strong people who value the importance of each other.

ASK YOURSELF

- What are your best habits? Worst habits?
- Have you noticed the habits of those around you?
- What are some habits that come naturally to you? The ones that take real effort?
- Who holds you accountable to those habits?

CHALLENGE

Find someone who struggles with the habits in which you excel. Help them. Find someone who excels with the habits in which you struggle. Ask them for help.

Building something great once doesn't make someone a builder. Instead, it's the their ability to successfully repeat the process.

SHOO FLY >>

There once was a young man named Sam who was known for asking a ton of questions in class. Some days, Sam would ask questions during the entire class; other days he would wait until the end. Frequently, he would ask questions that other students **wanted** to ask, but never did. More than often, his questions were viewed as annoying or repetitive. Additionally, he would arrive early to class and even stay a little late. He enjoyed this particular subject and the teacher who taught it.

To some, he wasn't a bother.

To most, he was considered as annoying as a little buzzing fly.

But one day, the professor assigned a group project. And of course, this young man whom many considered to be a nuisance became a commodity.

In nature, flies pollinate, identify good water, decompose, recycle, act as food source, and help gardeners more than they hurt. s annoying as flies can be, they do serve a purpose throughout nature. They can't help who they are and what they do.

The same can be said for the Sam in your group. Your Sam may come off as annoying. Your Sam may not ask too many questions, but instead be a slow thinker or talker. He may be a deep, detailed researcher, dotting every I and crossing every T. Whatever the case may be, the group must realize that he serves a purpose work tirelessly to see him as a commodity for the group.

Keep in mind that Sam is not the person who lacks etiquette, arrives late, leaves early and generates conflict. This person should, by all means, be shooed. (I'd even be okay with a swat or two.)

Sam is necessary—buzz and all. The next time you want to shoo the fly in your group, reconsider who that person might be.

ASK YOURSELF

- Who is the Sam in your group?
- What makes him annoying?
- What makes him a commodity?
- How would the group be without Sam?

CHALLENGE

Get to know Sam a little more. I bet there is more to him than what meets the eye.

Whatever the case may be, the group must realize every individual serves a purpose and work tirelessly to see each of them as a commodity for the group.

THE POWER OF WE >>
ME = WE (Part 1)

Conferences are always a joy...most of the time. Not so much the hustle and bustle of getting the product out or networking, but actually seeing what other professionals in your industry are doing. One thing that stood out to me at the last conference I attended, was an entrepreneur, alone on the stage, who never referenced himself as I. He discussed all that he went through and accomplished over the past year, yet always said we, not I.

Using we is important during the early stage of the company. Not necessarily because we have a lot of people directly involved in what we do, but eventually, we will. So, why not refer to them now? There are several reasons this is beneficial.

1. You'll soon have or be part of a team, so getting into the habit of referencing it is important.
2. People want to be a part of something that other people want to be a part of. If we talk about it as if others are already a part of it, people will want to join our team.
3. We can't teach others about a team, if we aren't a part of one?
4. We are not alone in our efforts (addressed more in Parts 2 and 3). Help should be extremely easy to identify if we are actually part of a team.
5. Using we is a subtle sign of humility and willingness to play well with (yield to) others.

We, in the truest since, is me. But by communicating otherwise, we speak into the future of our aspirations by including others in everything we say and do, even though they are not here yet.

This is the power of we.

ASK YOURSELF?

- Do you desire to work with others more closely?
- What steps are you taking to make that happen?
- What do those relationships look like?
- How can you present yourself as a viable and desirable teammate?

CHALLENGE

Often times, whether personally or professionally, people don't know what their company looks like in five or 10 years. Heck, next year is even a blur. Take some time and map out what **we** looks like for you and your company or group in the future.

People want to be a part of something that other people want to be a part of.

THE POWER OF WE >>
ME = WE (Part 2)

As discussed in Part 1 of "The Power of We," we identified why it is beneficial to reference yourself as we even though it's just you. This time we, will address the power of we from the perspective of having an actual team.

One of my previous jobs held a staff meeting once a week. During this meeting, the staff would sit in a circle and talk about their past, present or future activities. Each person would take turns speaking and identify other staff members he or she collaborated with along the way. When finished, the proverbial talking stick would pass to the next person.

However, it was always obvious when someone wasn't recognized for their contribution on a project. When this person received the talking stick, they would jokingly include himself in the project by bringing it back up. Nothing serious, yet it stood out enough to make the point: I contributed to that project as well.

Not everyone wants to be part of team. In fact, I bet there are a lot of people who would prefer to work individually. But when someone does contribute to a team effort, they want to be recognized. Good leaders recognize their team. Good leaders recognize their co-leaders. Good team members recognize other team members. Good team members recognize their leader. People outside of the team enjoy seeing recognition appropriately distributed among team members. When this happens—when people know their efforts will be acknowledged— they are more willing to contribute the next go-round.

This is the power of we.

ASK YOURSELF

- Can you name everyone in your group?
- Do you know their jobs?
- How many of these people do you work with regularly?
- How often do you highlight other individuals on your team or give them credit for their work?

CHALLENGE

Find new ways to be inclusive. Include individuals in your projects. Allow them to review and critique your projects. If you work alone, make an effort to build relationships with people who possess the skills that you hope to work with eventually. Then, after you've worked together, give thanks and recognition for their contribution.

When people know their efforts will be acknowledged— they are more willing to contribute the next go-round.

THE POWER OF WE >>
ME = WE (Part 3)

In Part 1, we established the importance of acknowledging the individual effort as we. Yes, we know it was just you because...well, it's only you. But that will not always be the case. So, get into the habit of talking from the team perspective.

In Part 2, we established the importance of acknowledging those who contribute toward the group effort. This is something that any participant within the group can and should do frequently. This leads us into the third and final power of we.

The power of we extends outside the group and further than we can imagine. But for time and length purposes, we will only address the two closest external contributors to the power of we. The first external contributors are the people who indirectly contribute to the group. These are the influences that come from outside the group and have loose attachments or affiliations to the people or goals of the team. This could be a mentor, editor, linear team (and any of its members) within the same company or peer professional. Anyone who provides feedback, encouragement, direction, input, etc., but are not considered a part of the group.

The second external contributors are the people who directly benefit from your service or product – the consumer. While this group is external, they are just as important as the group itself. One cannot exist without the other, so the consumer must be considered greatly.

Once all three areas are considered and valued as integral parts of the team effort, we takes on an entirely new perspective. We becomes much more important. We becomes much more relevant. We becomes much more pertinent. We begin to handle all aspects of the team with much more care. **We becomes much more powerful.**

This is the power of we.

ASK YOURSELF

- Who are your external contributors?
- How do you involve them in your internal processes?
- How much differently would your organization look without your external contributors?
- What are some of the most important things your external contributors have contributed?

CHALLENGE

If you do not have the external component to your we, find a few and include them in your internal processes. If you do have that component to your we, find more and different ways to use. They are invested in your success and want to see you do great things!

The power of we extends outside the group and further than we can imagine.

YiN-YANG >>

Chinese science and philosophy uses the concept of yin-yang to describe how opposites attract, connect, depend, and relate with and on each other. It is explained that these forces give way to each other to create balance in the world. In nature, this concept manifests in dark and light, high and low, hot and cold, fire and water, life and death, male and female, sun and moon, etc.

While explaining this concept, a philosopher said, "It is very important that water does not try to be or do what fire does. It is in being water that water fulfills its destiny within itself and completes its obligation to the world around it. The same with fire."

Likewise, being an effective team member means knowing who you are and how to contribute to the overall goal of the group. Once this is identified, you are required to be the best you and contribute the best way you know how. This is the epitome of teamwork—being able and willing to fit and flow within the yin and the yang of the group.

ASK YOURSELF

- What skill set do you bring to your group?
- Is it a skill that no one else brings to the group?
- What are the benefits of working with someone who complements your skill?
- Is there someone like that in your group? Who? How do they complement you?

CHALLENGE

Find someone you can complement and that complements you as well. Then figure out how you both can begin to work together. If you already work with them, find a way to work with them more.

Being an effective team member means knowing who you are and how to contribute.

CELEBRATE >>

I just finished watching "Celebrate," a music video directed by Sean C. Johnson. After listening to the song for the third time, the lyrics really start to settle in. These guys are telling their story, where they come from and what they've done. More than that, they are telling their listeners where they are and where they are going. And the theme they want everyone to walk away with is the concept of **celebrating** the process and progress of getting better.

How many times has a teammate or coworker been pigeonholed for something they did years ago? How many times has someone been unable to recover from a mistake they made when they were young or early into their career? You know how we do it.

"Don't give that project to ol' Johnny, you know he will [insert his mistake]."

"I wouldn't tell that to Susie, you know she has the tendency to [insert her shortcoming]."

Part of being an awesome team player is the ability to identify error, correct it and move on. Even more so, it means having the ability to **celebrate** the moment and the individual (or the team) when the error has been corrected. We don't **celebrate** each other enough. We are quick to point out flaws, but not as quick to give high-fives. And yes, people should do their jobs, mainly because it's their job. And yes, the old-school way says that you don't get **celebrated** for doing what you are supposed to do. And maybe there are people who don't constantly need to be **celebrated** for their accomplishments and achievements. But there are people who do need it and those around them must be willing to give it.

CELEBRATE the process. CELEBRATE progress. CELEBRATE each other.

ASK YOURSELF

- How well does your organization celebrate its team members?
- How well do you celebrate others?
- Do you like being celebrated?
- Do the people around you know that?

CHALLENGE

Start celebrating people for the smallest accomplishments. Notice how they respond. Repeat.

Part of being an awesome team player is the ability to identify error, correct it and move on.

HAND UP. HAND OUT. HAND DOWN. >>

One of my mentors is the senior pastor of what I believe to be one of the most sincere and effective churches in Oklahoma City. I was fortunate enough to spend three years serving in his church and among his people, having learned an extraordinary amount about service and relationship while under his tutelage. Their approach to attracting, developing and connecting members and reaching their community is the basis on which I build these next three sections.

We always should be aware that there is going to be someone before or after us who is smarter, faster and/or better than we.

HAND UP >>
(Part 1)

Relationship is often represented by the interlocking of hands. This is a universal sign of togetherness. When you interlock hands, one hand can't go anywhere without the other. Today, we are going to discuss the first of three ways hands interlock and the relationships they represent that everyone should have.

The first is the hand-up relationship which consists of having someone to whom you are always reaching for. This person is someone you admire or has something you want or need. This can be a mentor, pastor, supervisor, or manager. Whoever it is, they should be someone above you in the area you desire to grow. And while it can be someone removed from your close walk of life, it would be better to find someone you can hold hands with— literally. Meaning if you shake their hand and possibly even hug them frequently, they are close enough in your life to reach up, grab and hold.

Not only does this hand up give you immediate and direct access to years of hands-on experience and knowledge, it should also keep you humble. We always should be aware that there is going to be someone before or after us who is smarter, faster and/or better than we. They may be next door to us and we don't know. However, this becomes even more apparent when we can look them in the face and sit under their tutelage.

Lastly, the hand up should keep us moving forward or upward. When we have something to chase and pursue, we stay motivated. We continue to get out of bed looking for ways to get better at what we do. And if we find a hand up that follows this same line of reasoning, your hand up will always be helpful. At the moment they can no longer take you higher, a good hand up will pass you along to someone else who can continue to take you higher.

You should always have someone giving you a hand up.

ASK YOURSELF

- Who are the hand ups in your life?
- In which ways do they lift you up?
- Could you have made it to where you currently are without them?
- Think of one of your hand ups. Who is theirs?

CHALLENGE

Whoever is pulling you along or lifting you up obviously must be strong in a certain area and continues to have your best interest in mind. Take the time to express to them your appreciation for them and everything they do for you. You'd be surprised how far a thank you goes and how much more they'll pull you along for it.

We should always be aware that there is going to be someone before or after us who is smarter, faster and/or better than we are.

HAND OUT >>
(Part 2)

I really want you to get this in your head: Relationship is often represented by the interlocking of hands. This is a universal sign of togetherness. When you interlock hands, one hand can't go anywhere without the other. We've already discussed the importance of the hand up in part 1, and next we are going to discuss the second way hands interlock and the relationship it represents that everyone should have: hand OUT.

Traditionally, the hand out has been portrayed as a gesture of pity. However, in this case, it is defined as having someone who is linear to your walk of life. Someone with whom you can walk side-by-side, discuss, brainstorm, etc. More than likely, this is going to be a peer relationship, maybe a friend or co-worker. Someone who knows just as much as you do or has just as much experience. This isn't to say they aren't more experienced than you in other areas of life, but for the most part, it always equals out.

This relationship is good because it provides a safe place. The hand-out experience is where you receive encouragement, love, support and a mutual relationship where you give and receive. A relationship where you can let your hair down and kick off your shoes. You aren't necessarily trying to get anything (although you will), or give anything (although you will).

Lastly, the hand-out relationship is home base. These are the relationships that won't let you float away or sink. In a sense, they keep you grounded without holding you back. They can scratch your back and wipe your tears. They can lift your head to show you where you are supposed to be going when you are looking down at where you came from. They will not let you get discouraged because they will remind you of your dreams, goals, aspirations, ambitions and all the important stuff you'll need to hear when you feel like quitting.

You should always have someone in your life who has their hand out.

ASK YOURSELF

- Who are the hand outs in your life?
- In which ways do you interact with them?
- Could you have made it to where you currently are without them?
- Think of just one of your hand outs. To who else are they connected? How does that affect you?

CHALLENGE

Most often, the hand outs are the people who influence you the most. They are the people you hang out with the most. You probably bounce ideas off them the most. They provide the most feedback. Examine your closest co-workers, friends, business partners, and you'll probably be a nice mixture of them all. Are the people you're around who you want to be?

These are the relationships that won't let you float away or sink. In a sense, they keep you grounded without holding you back.

HAND DOWN >>
(Part 3)

Tired of it yet? I hope so. That means you almost got it. Here we go: Relationship is often represented by the interlocking of hands. This is a universal sign of togetherness. When you interlock hands, one hand can't go anywhere without the other. We've already discussed the importance of a hand up in part 1 and a hand out in part 2. Now we are going to discuss the third and final way hands interlock and the relationship it represents that everyone should have: hand DOWN.

The hand down, like the hand out, has such a negative connotation to it. Again, it is associated with pity and one person being beneath the other. And while there is an element to it, this must not be the heart of the gesture. In the same way we found someone to mentor us, we should find someone to do the same thing for, in the same manner. In fact, we should consider it a duty, an honor and a privilege to be in a position to help someone else get to where we are or where they want to be.

This relationship is also important because it reminds us of the part we play in the cycle of charity. There will always be someone better and smarter than us, but there will always be someone below or behind us. Once we realize this daunting truth, we find where we are in that cycle and immediately begin to reach up, out and down to grab hold of those around us. We tap into our community and surroundings to contribute whatever we can to process to ensure progress.

Lastly, reaching a hand down and helping someone up makes us stronger. In order to provide helpful, sound advice for someone finding their way, you must be confident and strong in your area of expertise. This also requires you possess certain traits that benefit the person you're helping. Traits like instinct, perseverance, hard work and dedication will allow you to reach a hand down to pull someone up.

ASK YOURSELF

- Who are the hand downs in your life?
- In which ways do you bring/lift them up?
- What was one of the more significant things you contributed to get them where they are today?
- Think of just one of your hand downs. Can you identify who their ups, outs and downs? How does that affect you?

CHALLENGE

When reaching down, we must remember someone once pulled us up. Reaching down isn't a sign of seniority or superiority. It's a sign of community and selflessness. Never forget to reach down and pull others along.

There will always be someone better and smarter than us, but there will always be someone below or behind us.

CASE OF THE MONDAYS >>

Why do Mondays get such a bad wrap? I'll tell you why: it's because people aren't excited about what Monday represents. For some, Monday represents the end of fun to their two-and-a-half-day party—a real perception for this group. For the remaining minority, Monday is an opportunity to continue or increase their fun. What's the difference between the two?

People who don't enjoy Mondays either 1) dislike what they do, 2) would rather perhaps do something else, or 3) dislike their co-workers. As an employer or team member, there is very little you can do about any of these reasons, but the little you <u>can</u> do must be done.

What are those little things that can be done?

Well, the truth of the matter is the things you will end up doing aren't little at all. In fact, they are extremely large gestures toward your employees that many companies normally don't do. Those things have to do with creating a comfortable, welcoming environment that reinforces the company motto, mission or philosophy. The way to create this environment is:

1. Invest in the physical environment. Soothing colors, encouraging posters or quotes, comfortable chairs, soft music, calming light, etc. will make sure people are relaxed and can do their job without physical distractions. Anything additional you do to spice up the place is a bonus.

2. Invest in the professional environment. Encourage healthy (i.e. frequent + clear + open = successful) communication. Invest in the learning process of the team. Make sure they have the creative equipment

and tools needed to do their job as best as possible. Invest whatever is needed in order the get the best professional "them" to work every day.

3. Invest in the social environment. People not only need to appreciate the physical and creative work space, but they need to like the people with whom they work. The number one thing people value about their jobs (and miss when they leave) is the people they work with. (Number two is the consistent paycheck. Number three is the structure/schedule.) The truth of the matter is people don't normally enter the work environment hating or liking the people on their team. Employers usually let that process develop over time. Instead, employers should intentionally influence this process by directing it in a positive direction instead of trying to pull it back once it has already turned negative.

The same applies to you as an employee. Your employer isn't completely responsible for investing in the physical, professional and social environments. You must contribute as well. Just think of the parent who provides what appears to be the perfect living environment for the child who turns out...not so perfect. Or the school who provides the perfect learning environment for the student who turns out...less than stellar. Or the spouse who attempts to be the perfect mate and his or her partner cheats anyways. Your employer and the environment is only part of the solution. You must want to be there. You must take advantage of every opportunity. They will set the tone. You bring the flavor.

Let's destroy the Monday myth and turn the work week into an extension of the weekend.

ASK YOURSELF

- Are you a Monday person? Why or why not?
- What would make Mondays better at your job?
- How would you go about implementing those suggestions?
- Why do you not think those suggestions have not been implemented before?

CHALLENGE

Ideally, organizations would be invested in making their employees and work environments happy and healthy. However, regardless if they do or not, it is up to the individual to decide how their Monday will go. Decide that every Monday is going to be awesome and begin making steps to ensure you protect your Monday vibe.

People don't normally enter the work environment hating or liking the people on their team.

TOUCH >>

One of the skills I desire the most is learning how to handle people. Not handle them in a manipulative or advantageous manner, but knowing how to use that tender touch to make every aspect of our encounter a pleasant one. If you've ever encountered an individual with this skill, the experience is unmistakable and unforgettable. I believe this amazing touch can be summed up in two concepts: how you handle people and how you handle difficult situations.

People want respect. They want to be heard, validated, understood, remembered...all of that stuff. The person who can accomplish that will leave a lasting impression on everyone they encounter. Of course, this skill isn't acquired haphazardly. This tender touch requires an intentional effort and an immense amount of practice. It requires selflessness and the ability to intentionally appreciate, desire and pursue the bigger picture.

Situations are just as complex. And because they vary in so many ways, there is no cookie-cutter way to approach them all. Of course, when considering any situation, one must know that the entire situation must be handled in the same manner, as people are often attached to these difficult situations. People who desire to handle these situations with a tender touch can't over react; they must respond appropriately. And this isn't necessarily because this is what they <u>want</u> to do, but because they know it's what needs to be done. (I can only assume the right/proper/appropriate response becomes the initial response over time.)

This attribute isn't only found in candy-carrying church ladies. It's not only found in the wise pipe-smoking grandpa. There are all kinds of people who possess this quality. And if you've met someone like this, I guarantee that person has touched your life and still remains in your mind and heart.

ASK YOURSELF

- How would you describe your people touch: Rough? Gentle?
- How would others describe your people touch?
- Do you know someone who handles people they way you wish you could? What kind of touch do they have?
- Have you ever been handled in a way that made you angry? Feel pleasant? How is your current relationship with that person(s)?

CHALLENGE

When handling other people, it becomes more about them and less about us. True, we want to protect ourselves. True, it's hard taking the high road. But the greatest leaders most frequently adhere to the needs of others, put others before themselves and make a practice of servitude. When all is said and done, handle people well, handle situations well and you'll have a good handle on everything else.

People want respect. They want to be heard, validated, understood, remembered.

WORK SHOULD COME SECOND >>

But that's why we are here, right? To work, get stuff done, make money, reach goals, accomplish....stuff. Work, work, work! Right?!

I agree....kind of. Of course, work is the common thread that brought your group together. Without the job, there would be no group. I understand. The job is about completing a task. However, it is just as important to understand the dynamics of HOW the work gets done. The how includes three components: 1) the individual, 2) the group and 3) the kind of work. The attitude and success of the group is determined by these three components.

In the same manner that each puzzle piece is significant to the entire puzzle, the individual is important to the group. Whether it's an athletic team, assembly line, leadership team or wait staff, the individual must be considered beyond their isolated responsibilities. Are they fast or slow? Quiet or talkative? Educated or skilled? Early riser or night owl? Leader or follower? Organized or jumbled? Team player or loner? The combination of these characteristics contributes to the culture and success of the group.

The group is simply the combination of individuals. The feel of the group will be determined by how these individuals interact. And while individuals are expected to be professional within the work environment, there are steps that can be taken in creating an environment that allows the group to be most successful. This is where the dynamics of the group become a factor, addressing them becomes a means to building, and the ability to perfect them becomes an attribute and a tool.

Lastly, the kind of work must be considered when gathering individuals into a group. Is the work stressful or relaxed? Will efforts be mostly interactive or isolated? Is the concept of a team even necessary to complete the task? These are all significant components to consider in a group setting as they will determine the functionality and direction of the group.

Listen, if it was just about the work itself, groups would pursue the fastest, brightest and smartest people to do the job. These individuals would be able to slide into the group and eventually attain the utopian group dynamics that rarely exist in a group setting. Instead, employers, coaches, supervisors, managers, and CEOs consider the skill, but are just as interested, if not more, in the person, their personality and characteristics.

I believe the groups that focus on work second are the best and most successful groups. This is why I say, consider the person first and let the work follow suit.

ASK YOURSELF

- Have you ever worked with someone who was skilled, but socially inept?
- How did this person fit into the social dynamics of the group?
- Have you ever been a part of a group in which you didn't fit? What was it like?
- What are some other reasons you believe social dynamics are essential to group work?

CHALLENGE

Spend some time bonding with your team outside of your job requirements. It is often in those areas where deeper and more functional relationships are formed and professional duties become easier and more fluid.

WE NEED YOU! >>

I was sitting in Starbucks with one of my mentors. As the conversation was coming to a close, he asked about my new church home. *Was I fitting in? Had I found a place to be active?* As my demeanor changed, I fiddled with my cup, tapped the table and began to reply with a myriad of doubts and concerns. He looked through all those excuses I gave him and simply said, "You must be afraid." I must have answered with a confused look on my face because he began to expound on his reply. "You are afraid that your ideas won't work or that they'll use you up or you won't be accepted or they'll take your ideas. Or you must be afraid of the work that will be required to implement your ideas or serve in a particular capacity. Or you're afraid you'll give your soul only to receive a pat on the back. Whatever the case, you're afraid." And to his credit, I was. Fear was at the root of all my concerns. However, what happened next was completely unexpected. My mentor started ranting on encouragement. It completely changed my perspective. And while I can't quote him exactly, it went something like this:

I know it doesn't seem like it most of the time. I know they may not say it as much as they should or could, but I'll say it for them now: We need you. We need your energy, ideas, effort, constructiveness and focus. And we don't need a shell of you. We need all your awesomeness! We need the best of you! The Derrick de la Derrick! We don't want the weekend's leftovers. We don't want your shattered fragments of doubt. We don't have room for your crumbs of self-consciousness. We need the new and improved YOU! The you that is selflessly dedicated to the cause. The inspired and invigorated version of yourself. And we don't just want your skill, we want the infectious fuel behind the fire that makes you burn with passion. We need your optimism, your wit, your humor and lightheartedness. We need your creativity. We need the best version of yourself that you can give and then we want more. Because you have it. And the more you share it, the better it gets, the more people benefit from it, the more the team can do with it, the better we are from working with it. And...do I need to keep going?.... because I can....

As he was talking, I could immediately feel the physical and emotional boost from this encouragement. I was amazed and had forgot how good it felt to have someone believing in me.

I'm not saying people should need a pep talk in order to function optimally. In fact, part of being a functional and mature team player is being able to encourage yourself to complete a task and effectively contribute by whatever means and in whatever setting. However, every now and then, people need to hear how awesome they are, how much they are appreciated and how much they are needed. They need to know and hear what their peers and leaders think about them. They need to refill their reservoir of confidence that has simply been depleted by the wear-and-tear of life and duty. The small investment of encouragement can go a long way. Everyone, without exception, will eventually need this tender touch of encouragement.

To you, I say the same thing. It may not seem like it. Your team and/or boss may not say it as much as they could or should. But, you are awesome. There is no one else on earth who has your unique makeup. You are one of a kind. And while there may be people who do what you do, they can't do it like you do it. They don't have your flair or your quirk. Your team.....they need you.

ASK YOURSELF

- When was the last time someone filled your heart with encouragement?
- Who was it? How did they do it? Do you remember what they said?
- When was the last time you encouraged someone?
- Why is encouragement important?

CHALLENGE

Contact someone right now who has been a little down lately. You know, the one you keep saying you will contact soon, but never do. Do it. Now. Text them. Email them. Facebook message them. Tweet them. By whatever means, do it now. And encourage them like never before.

I know it doesn't seem like it most of the time. I know they may not say it as much as they should or could, but I'll say it for them now: We need you.

PLAY TiME >>

I can tell when my wife and I haven't had fun and played in a while. We get cranky and irritable. Everything the other person says is misinterpreted. The environment surrounding our relationship isn't fun.

And this doesn't just apply to marriage. It fits any other group I'm a part of as well. I was able to tell when my college football team wasn't having fun. We'd start losing and then the finger pointing would begin. The same would apply with my classmates in college. The vibe was different when we enjoyed an assignment or were able to experience success in our projects. The same applied for the fitness center at which I worked for eight years. I could tell when tension was high and we had worked for an extended period of time without playing together. Our creativity would decline dramatically. Everyone would begin to nit-pick. Office doors would close. Everyone would become an island.

Playing has the ability to drown out the components of real life, even if for a moment. It allows for relationships to lightened, yet deepened at the same time. It relieves stress and creates a social bond around more positive experiences. Play time is an important—no, it is an essential component to every significant relationship around you and to whichever group you belong. Make sure you make play time a priority.

ASK YOURSELF

- Is your group intentional about scheduling play time?
- What does your play time look like?

- Who could decide whether the group needs play time?
- What does it look like when your group is all work and no play?

CHALLENGE

Create a schedule that includes play time, even if it's just for you. Schedule play time at work and at home, with your friends and family. In whatever group, in whatever setting, there should always be time for play.

Playing has the ability to drown out the components of real life, even if for a moment.

RED ROVER, RED ROVER >>

I once heard a professor compare acquiring leaders to creating leaders. It was an interesting concept. He compared buy in, integration, longevity, commitment and familiarity. After listening to his comparison, I believed I would rather create leaders. Or so I thought.

BUY IN

When creating leaders, are they more likely to buy into the company's culture and philosophy? I believe so. Of course, I only have my experience to pull from. I know how it felt when someone from outside the group was placed in leadership, rather than the position being filled from within. The outside person didn't know the ropes. They didn't know the energy of the group. Of course, they could learn all of these things. They could have easily bought into the culture and philosophy, but there were people there who had already bought in.

Then, the *perception* of buy in was directly related to whether the group believed the new person would be able to integrate into the company. Are they willing to adjust or do they expect everyone to change for them? Can they become accustomed to the leadership styles of the people to which they report? Can they account for the learning and working styles of the people that will report to them? Consider their personal working and learning style. Will it fit well in whatever group they are placed? I'm sure the hiring manager considered these questions and had full confidence in their abilities. However, there were people already there who were integrated into the system and culture. Why not hire them?

The same process could be repeated with longevity, commitment and familiarity, but the same insecurities and possibilities will still exist by the group in which the new leader is placed. No one will know how well the outsider fits until they've been given the opportunity to fit. On the flip side, the people who didn't get the leadership position will wonder why they weren't picked. Maybe none of the existing applicants within the group were qualified for the position. Maybe leadership wanted a different perspective, so they brought in someone from the outside. There are several possibilities, but I can say whatever the reason, the goal is to make the group stronger.

This reminds me of the game Red Rover. I was always the guy who was pleased with the initial team I picked. I thought adding people could possibly weaken the team. Besides, I picked my team on purpose and according to their skills. I was meticulous about the people I picked. But the game calls for people to be added so the team can grow in size and in strength. It's unavoidable. You MUST add people to your team.

My conclusion? While I'm still partial to creating leaders, both acquiring and creating are essential. There are going to be times when bringing in someone new is best. There are going to be times when grooming an existing member of the group meets the need. It is up to leadership to make that decision and the team to make sure they do their part so everyone succeeds.

RED ROVER, RED ROVER, WHO DO YOU PLAN TO CALL OVER?

- Have you ever been in line for a position and was overlooked by someone from outside of your department or the company?
- Have you ever been brought into a group and promoted over others who were in line for the position?

- What do you think are the main differences between those experiences?
- Outside of the things listed above, in what other ways can you justify hiring from within or bringing in someone from outside the group?

CHALLENGE

We have discussed this from the individual's perspective, but we have not discussed how something like this may affect the group. 1) Consider a position you would like to hold. 2) Find someone who hires for that position. 3) Ask them about their decision-making process for hiring internally versus externally.

The game calls for people to be added so the team can grow in size and in strength.

TWEETABLE >>

It is said that the modern attention span stores information in tweetable amounts. What's a tweetable amount? It is 140 characters. What's a character? It is any part of the sentence that fills a space, including letters, numbers and punctuation.

And as a reference, the above section wouldn't be tweetable. It would have been two tweets!

I remember sitting in church for hours when I was younger. No exaggeration. Literally **hours**! And my mother would dare me to go to sleep. If guests were present or it was a special church service, it was raised to a double dare. To this day, I'm still not sure if she was trying to make sure I was listening or if she didn't want to be embarrassed by my snoring. It could be both. Whatever the case, she expected me to be alert the entire time. She would even ask me questions about the sermon during the car ride home. And if I didn't know any of the answers, she'd reply, "I bet you know the answers to [insert whatever show I was watching or video game I was playing at that time]." I'd reply (in my head, of course), *I'd remember it if it wasn't so long and boring.*

Church for me then equals meetings, emails and soapboxes for the millennials now.

Communication is a delicate exchange of information between the sender and receiver. Interpretation fills the space between them. External and internal variables influence the way that information is sent, received and interpreted. This means, the sender must be aware of much more than delivering information.

Look, I get it. I understand why people are appalled

at the vast decline of communication. But I also understand the growing support for trimming the fat from communication. While both sides could debate, resist and persist, the trend of shortened and more direct communication will continue to grow despite the mild resistance.

With that in mind, I suggest all leaders adapt to the advancing technology and new means of communication by transforming their long-winded efforts to communicate in tweetable amounts. Your Generation X'ers and millennials will thank you with more direct and effective communication in return. (Nope, that wasn't tweetable either.)

ASK YOURSELF

- How do you feel when listening to someone who is long-winded?
- How do you feel when listening to someone didn't speak long enough?
- How do you feel when listening to someone who spoke perfectly in content and length?
- Do you prefer shorter or longer forms of communication? Does it depend on the topic or setting?

CHALLENGE

Practice being intentional when communicating. Make sure your thoughts are clear and concise, but be able to expand them if necessary. Be able to distinguish the difference between concise and incomplete, between exhaustive and necessarily elaborate. The difference can make or break your story, presentation, proposal or bid.

The sender must be aware of much more than delivering information.

KNOCK KNOCK >>

Does the open-door policy really work? It's supposed to make team members feel like they can come into their leader's office anytime. So, in a sense, it does work if simply getting people in the door is the goal. But I think when people use the term open-door policy, they are trying to <u>infer</u> open lines of communication. And we all know that an open door doesn't mean open communication. It literally means, *You can come into my office or feel free to disturb me, or that what I'm doing at this moment isn't important enough for me to close my door because if it was, the door would be closed which means...don't come in.*

Maybe the open door says, "you can come in, but I won't necessarily come out." Meaning, *You can ask, but I can't promise any answers.* This is one of the many things that makes transparent communication tricky. The one with the information has all the power. Or is the one with all of the power the one who has the information? Hmm....

Either way (or both ways), the open-door policy is deceiving. Communication must be intentional, practiced, and honest, and individuals must become proficient in several styles of communication. Otherwise, the open-door policy means something other than what it traditionally suggests, which is open communication.

ASK YOURSELF

- What do you think of when you hear open-door policy?
- Have you ever had to use the open-door policy?

What was it like?
- Do you have an open-door policy? At work? At home? In relationships?
- What is the work environment like when there is not an open-door policy?

CHALLENGE

Different groups of people and different scenarios require different levels of transparency. Consider those different people and different scenarios and decide early where those lines are drawn. This will help you stick to your guns, be prepared and ready when conflict arises.

Communication must be intentional, practiced, and honest.

RULE OF THREES >>

If one doesn't exist, it should. I definitely know it's a social phenomenon. (I think.) My wife pats her sandwich three times before eating it. I usually have to tell my kids something three times before they get it. There are three parts of a day: morning, noon and night. A three-strand cord is not easily broken. Speaking of chords, I love three-part harmony. Sheldon (a character on Big Bang Theory) knocks three times on every door. I can get a meal at McDonald's for a little over $3. Earth is the third planet from the sun. I usually feel sore after the third push-up.

Okay, maybe there isn't a rule of threes, but I think repetition is what I was going for.

A professor once told me I'd be convinced on the third time. "Third time of what?" I replied. He said, "Of everything." While I'm sure this isn't a hard and fast rule within the universe, what I took from it was repetition. Getting better requires repetition. No matter the job or the skill, doing it over and over and over again moves you toward perfection. This can apply to an individual or a group. The things that are going to make you better must be done often. The same applies to any group. The more those things are done, the more natural they become.

Think about it: waking up early, eating healthy, exercising, writing, singing—all those things require repetition. And this is just my list. This doesn't include all of the things YOU want to work on. You may want to lower your Rubik's cube time. Or keep the lines straight in your grass. Or become better at thinking more positive thoughts. You may want to lower your golf score. Or memorize the periodic table. Absolutely nothing worth doing can escape the need for repetition.

So, I say to you: you may not be convinced on the third time, but if you want to do it well, keeping doing it. It'll happen. It'll come through.

ASK YOURSELF

- What's an area in which you'd like to become better, but don't pay it enough attention?
- What is something you're pretty good at doing because of practice?
- Do you think you could help someone else become just as good as you in that area?
- What happens when you don't practice at something you were once good at doing?

CHALLENGE

What's your "thing?" Go do it! If you don't have a thing, find one then go do it! And do it frequently.

Getting better requires repetition.

PARTY POOPER >>

You know the guy: the one who has to go against the happy grain. He's the one who refuses to be happy when everyone else is, sits in the corner at the office party, sends a gift instead of coming to the celebration, doesn't come because he can't wear his jeans, refuses to put his hands up at the concert, grabs the remote because it's his house. You know the guy! The party pooper!

This guy shouldn't be confused with the level-headed, reserved and cautious individual. This person is usually non-confrontational and really wants the best for the group instead of simply wanting attention, like the pooper, who is generally selfish, stubborn and bad for business.

For any group trying to move forward, grow and get better together, the pooper must either get on board or be removed. People can genuinely understand and accept caution, but not conflict and sourness. A wise man once said that a little poop ruins the entire batch of brownies. Ha! So true!

Every party has a pooper, just make sure it isn't you.

ASK YOURSELF

- Who is the pooper of your group?
- Are they always the pooper or is it situational?
- What steps do you take to include this person?
- How does their poop impact the rest of the group?

CHALLENGE

It's easy to ignore or exclude the pooper. Next time that person gets in a funk, decide to find a way to include that person at all costs—even if it's at the inconvenience of the entire group. If the gesture doesn't speak volumes, it may be a sign that the situation requires a little more attention than just an invite.

The pooper must either get on board or be removed.

THE BIG-PICTURE TEAM >>

Growing up, my father was a stickler on the way I treated my mother. As a result, my childhood had a heavy dose of saying "yes ma'am," holding doors, pulling out chairs, removing my hats, standing so she could sit and hauling heavy stuff. I didn't know it then, but my dad had the bigger picture in mind. He knew what kind of man he wanted me to be as an adult. Fast forward about 20 years, and I still hold doors, stand so she can sit, say "yes ma'am" and lift heavy stuff.

Again, my dad focused on the small things with the bigger picture in mind.

My dad also loved puzzles. He would approach them in the strangest of ways, yet he always completed them. No matter the size or number of pieces, at the end of the puzzle, we all eventually saw the BIG PICTURE. I can see him now, hunched over the table with his glasses barely hanging on the tip of his nose. Every once in a while, he would reach his right hand over to the right edge of the table, grab his glass of tea, take a gulp and simultaneously, set the glass down while rubbing his left-hand thumb across his forehead, gathering sweat and slinging it across the room. Puzzle time was intense. I would try to help him, but would often times slow down the process. I wouldn't group the colors together or match the edges or create the smaller pictures first, which were all his approaches. He had a process in creating the big picture. After I would get frustrated, in the most encouraging way that he could muster in the moment, he would always say, "You can't create the big picture without placing the smaller pieces."

There's nothing wrong with being the big idea person or the big picture team. However, you can't be so big picture that you neglect the smaller pieces. Another way of saying it: you can't be such a big picture person that you neglect the smaller picture people.

Big picture people say things like, *Don't sweat the small stuff. Like a turtle, let it roll off your back. If it's maggot-sized, it'll eventually fly away. Be a bee and ignore the buzz. Take it all as a grain of salt. Don't miss the forest looking at the trees. Don't let one moment determine your entire life.* (I am usually this guy.)

Small picture people say things like, *Discipline is in the details. Crawl before you walk. Don't put the cart before the horse. Let's make sure we dot every "I" and cross every "T." Let's look at it one more time.* (This is usually my wife.)

If teams aren't careful, the picture process can be a huge obstacle toward cohesion, and be a substantial point of conflict. In order to progress effectively through the picture process, groups must realize, like my dad and wife, that big pictures are made of smaller pictures. Dreamers need people to put hands and feet to their vision. Visionaries need decisionaries. One doesn't exist without the other. There is no right or wrong way to approach the picture process. Everyone just needs to be on the same page about what is being created and how it is going to be created. If this is the approach, every team can be a BIG PICTURE team.

ASK YOURSELF

- Who are the big picture people in your group?
- Who are the small picture people in your group?
- Does your group create space for both kinds of people within the group?
- What happens in a group with only small or big picture people?

CHALLENGE

What kind of picture person are you? The next time you are in a meeting or discussing a project, make sure picture people opposite of you are heard.

You can't create the big picture without placing the smaller pieces.

HOW ARE YOUR CONNECTIONS? >>

Too often, when it comes to relationships, we confuse frequency and proximity with quality. Just because I interact with someone often does not mean those are quality encounters. Just because we office together does not mean we are friends. Keep in mind, I don't want to devalue frequency and proximity, as those are positive components to all successful relationships, but they can't be the only components.

So, how do we measure those encounters? How do we evaluate the connections we have with our spouse, children, friends, parents, siblings, coworkers or any other person or group with whom we interact?

Since all of those relationships are going to vary from person to person and group to group, I can't give you a concrete scale or an approach that works across the board. However, I can say with confidence, which ever method you choose should be done often and with improving your connection in mind.

For example, reflection and evaluation shouldn't be done only when something has gone wrong in a relationship. If evaluating your connection is done often, it will prevent those issues before they get a chance to take root and manifest. When reflecting, you are often able to catch subtle things that were missed in the moment. I can't imagine the number of marriages and friendships that could have been saved with reflection and evaluation. What about the amount of money companies waste training new employees because of attrition and poor retention as a result of eroded relationships? What about the churches that wouldn't have split? What about the numerous bipartisan efforts that have been halted? Proximity and frequency are deceptive. If the connections are intentional and quality is a focus, they will grow and thrive.

That said, how are your connections?

ASK YOURSELF

- Have you been betrayed by someone you talk to and hang out with often?
- Have you ever tried to befriend someone who didn't want to befriend you?
- What did either/both of those feel like?
- With them and others, how did you modify your behavior going forward?

CHALLENGE

Often times, people hesitate to be direct in relationships. Be more intentional in your relationships. Let people know what you think, what you expect, where they stand with you and where you want that relationship to go. It'll save you time and create clarity between you and the people around you.

If evaluating your connection is done often, it will prevent those issues before they get a chance to take root and manifest.

SPEED LiMiT >>
(Part 1)

I must admit: I'm not the most patient driver. In fact, I'm probably the driver most of the other drivers hate. I get annoyed by people who drive the speed limit and are only slightly tolerable of those who barely drive over the speed limit. I despise red lights. Yellow lights are indicators to speed up before the red light comes. A stream of green lights usually means the rest of my day will be great! I try my best to avoid traffic formations — you know, the group of cars that refuse to allow the cars behind them to pass. (I can only assume this is to prove a point or teach a lesson.) Like I said, I'm not the most patient driver.

Unfortunately, I tend to be this person off the road as well.

Waiting on others is hard. For me, being patient is a conscious decision. With my children, wife, and friends, I've had to learn to live at the pace of the group. At work, in church, and during board games, I've learned to play at the pace of the group. When I eat—Man, when I eat! I've learned to eat at the pace of the group.

Of course, there are going to be some who think that when the group is slow, they should speed up. And that could be the case at times. There are definitely those who provide a spark when one is needed. Then there are those who think the group is moving too fast and they need to slow down. This is also applicable, as there are those who ground and level the group. Whatever the case, the pace is never going to be perfect for everyone. But a part of finding the speed limit of the group is to make sure the group is traveling at a pace that is safe, productive and fitting for the majority involved. And those who can't obey the speed limit, may arrive at their destination only to notice they are alone and everyone dislikes them.

The speed limit is set for a reason. Find it and follow it.

ASK YOURSELF

- What are three areas in which you can grow in patience?
- Can you think of a time when you were the fast one of the group? How did that feel?
- Can you think of a time when you were the slow one of the group? How did that feel?
- Can you think of a time when everyone was going the same speed (on the same page)? How did you/ everyone feel?

CHALLENGE

Be intentional about finding the pace of the group. In fact, be the pacesetter.

BONUS

Groups are the most productive when everyone is on the same page. BUT being on the same page doesn't always mean working at the same speed. Sometimes, being on the same page means working at different paces. The most important part is everyone working together, understanding their speed (whether fast or slow), and toward the same goal.

Waiting on others is hard. The pace is never going to be perfect for everyone.

SPEED LiMiT >>
(Part 2)

When it comes to the pace of the group, the speed limit needs to be adhered and not ignored. When the speed limit is obeyed, the group is allowed to progress and operate safely and productively. And while there may be times the group travels above or below their normal speed limit, the normal pace will be what works – whatever that looks like. The most important thing is that everyone must intentionally travel the designated pace.

What does it look like when individuals go rogue and begin driving recklessly? Well, this is when accidents happen, vehicles are damaged and lives are lost. And what does this look like in a group setting?

Think about the last time you were a part of a group and someone exhibited road rage. I'm sure the group worked to establish a plan and course of action. Then someone, who probably wasn't on board with the initial plan, decides to violate the group's trust and implement their own process instead—<u>without</u> the permission or approval of the group. While there are times when this may happen and success may occur (which rarely happens), it only takes that one incident for trust to be lost.

Don't get me wrong. I don't want you to read this and take it as a plea for conformity or a sheepish approach. There are some instances where an individual may be required to exceed the normal pace of the group. There may even be an occurrence when the decision to do so must be made without consulting the group. This is the exception and not the rule. When I decide to get into the vehicle with a person, I expect to arrive at our destination safely. Additionally, others should be hurt in the process and the limits should be obeyed. The same applies for group work. There are rules and protocol. Anything and everything that is accomplished should be and can be done within those parameters.

I know...I know. It isn't sexy, but it's proven.

The speed limit is set for a reason. Find it and follow it.

ASK YOURSELF

- Can you think of a time when someone in your group went rogue?
- What were the consequences?
- If good, would you encourage this behavior more frequently?
- If bad, how can groups prevent this from happening again?

CHALLENGE

Going rogue should not be seen as an admirable, impulsive surge in creativity or liberty for exploration. Those moments should be presented to and decided on by the group. As much as you may want to, DON'T GO ROGUE! No matter how slow or fast the group is going. Hang in there. You don't want to arrive at your destination with a trail of destruction behind you.

The speed limit is set for a reason.
Find it and follow it.

TENERGY >>

Yes. I just made up a word...I think. It is a one-word descriptor I like to use when describing the concept of "team plus energy" (team + energy). Think about it. There's the energy one person brings to the group. Then, there's the combined energy of all of the individual energies. THEN, there's the energy that comes from outside the group, when the energy from inside the group becomes infectious.

Still don't get it? Let's use a good ole fashioned Oklahoma Thunder basketball game as an example. There's the energy ~~Kevin Durant~~ Russell Westbrook brings to the team. There's the energy other players bring to the team as well. THEN, there's impact the home crowd has on the home team when they see the individual and collective energies from the team. When all of these components are included in a team effort, you get the amazing concept of tenergy. It is the combined energy of all the individuals within a group. In the case of the OKC Thunder, a group effort consists of the players, coaching staff, team administration and fans.

Can't relate to the Oklahoma City Thunder? Let's use your office. You know who the energizer bunny is and you know the sloth. You know the one who comes up with the idea, then delivers and the one who is the last one on board. You know the person who communicates clearly and effectively and the person who says "uhhhhhhhhhh" in between each incoherent thought. People being a certain type and energy to the group. When those energies are combined, you get tenergy.

Of course, the components will vary when applying

this comparison to your specific group, but the concept stays the same. In the business world, there are several components that make up a group. In order for the energy to remain high, everyone must be on the same page and contribute their best effort in the way that's most effective for the group. If this isn't done consistently, tenergy can also work in the opposite direction as well. The same way positive tenergy can snowball into something great and successful, it also has the possibility to grow into something negative and destructive. We've all seen what happens when bad energy infects a group—morale sinks, blame is passed, responsibility is fumbled and trust is forgotten. (The Thunder fans have seen this manifest over the last few seasons.)

Although team energy is a big picture concept, it can't snowball into something great without the contributions of the smaller flakes. Smaller flakes = YOU! This means every individual has to commit to the team. What does this commitment look like? It looks like showing up each and every day ready to contribute your best effort and your best energy to the group. If negativity is brought through the door, it should be seen as an opportunity to address and eliminate that particular issue, so the group can grow closer and go further together.

Tenergy. You can't build a team without it.

ASK YOURSELF

- Who are the high-energy contributors in your group?
- Who are the low-energy contributors in your group?
- What kind of contributor are you?
- How would you describe the energy level of your group?

CHALLENGE

Be the spark!

REMEMBER ME?! >>

I absolutely hate when this happens. When someone remembers you, but you don't remember them. Of course, there are several levels to this encounter. You remember their face, but not their name. (This is magnified when they remember your name.) Maybe the name rings a bell, but you can't remember their face. Maybe you remember the name, but in your mind, their face isn't the face you attached to the name. Even worse, you have absolutely no idea who they are, but they are sharing several encounters you've had together. Or (last one, promise) you check your social media outlets and you <u>are</u> friends or follow each other. There are very few social situations that make me uncomfortable. This is one.

And while being the person who doesn't remember may feel awkward, imagine how it feels being the one not remembered. I've been there. It sucks. I know that people meet tons of people. I also know it is unfair to expect you to meet everyone who crosses your path. But to be confident enough in your past interactions to address someone—and they not remember you? Ouch! No one would ever say it, but it's like saying, "Our interaction wasn't important enough for me to remember you or the interaction." OUCH! And I bring this up, not so much for names and faces, but more for validation.

Remembering names, faces, stories and experiences validates people. No, it doesn't validate their career or profession, but it validates them as a person. It lets them know they matter on some kind of level. I wonder the number of endorphins released within the body when someone hears their name, is the center of a funny story, is recognized, is called pretty/handsome or is told their presence was enjoyed. I don't have the exact number, but from personal experience, it feels great! Everyone can identify with that feeling. It's absolutely wonderful! And in so many words, it says, "That person and our interaction was worth remembering." The thought of forever being etched in someone's memory has to be flattering.

I worked for a company whose CEO not only remembered faces and names, but also personal details and even high school mascots. When people recall how interacting with him made them feel, they would light up with amazement and surprise. But he would personally approve every single new hire and would spend time getting know every employee before they began working for the company. This company had anywhere from 2,500 to 4,000 employees on campus at any given time. Talk about having a good memory and being committed to knowing and "seeing" people.

The concept of remembering is a major component within teams and groups. Why? Groups are more than people gathered for goal-oriented purposes. Groups are extended circles of life in which individuals become invested, not only professionally, but also socially, physically, mentally, emotionally, and sometimes, spiritually. For this reason, we should be quick to remember the journey of the group and contributions of its individuals along the way. People want to know they are appreciated and valued. What other way to validate that claim than to take time to remember them?

ASK YOURSELF

- What are some factors that prevent us from remembering details about people?
- What are some practical steps you can take to remember people better?

- What are a few relational benefits to remembering people?
- What are some possible setbacks to not remembering people?

CHALLENGE

Take time to tell someone something positive and meaningful about them every day. This will indicate your interest in them as an individual. It may be easier to start with friends and family.

Remembering names, faces, stories and experiences validates people. No, it doesn't validate their career or profession, but it validates them as a person.

PAiN >>
(Part 1)

I'm sure pain would be at the top of the list of reasons why people don't like to work in groups. Well, maybe not the word pain, but the discomfort of working in group settings. You could probably reference your own group experiences and agree with my assumption (hopefully not).

Let's expand it a bit more.

An example could be people not pulling their own weight, leading you to do most, if not all, of the work. Maybe you held your ground and demanded everyone else pull their weight, in which you, as an individual, succeeded on principle and completion of work, but the group failed. Maybe it was easier to work by yourself instead of coordinating and communicating to ensure every aspect of the project was completed. Then, there are the avoidance issues that come with group work, in which you fear that being short and direct will come off as cold with the inability to work well with others. Whatever decision you make stems from wanting to avoid the pain that usually accompanies working with other people.

With this is mind, I'll refer to the muscle as an example.

There's a certain amount of "pain" expected when trying to make a muscle stronger. The same is expected when using a muscle that hasn't been used in a while. It's going to hurt. Why? Because muscles use resistance as a means to grow big and strong. The same applies to developing muscles as a group. When developing a group—trying to make it stronger—there is a certain amount of pain or resistance one should expect. However, this pain shouldn't occur for pain's sake. It should take place for the purpose of building muscle. Yes, you are going to be using certain parts of the group that haven't been used frequently or correctly. But the hope is that you'll experience less pain with that particular muscle group the more you use them. In turn, that particular part of the body will be stronger and will operate more efficiently.

Let's say it a different way. For instance, if your group has terrible communication, you all need to learn how to communicate in order to get better and stronger. If your group has low follow through, they are going to have to meticulously follow a project through from start to finish until they learn how to do it in their sleep. The same goes for conflict, budgets, chain of command, marketing, etc. In whatever your group is horrible, you are going to have to do that thing on purpose, the right way, until you are proficient.

I know it's uncomfortable, but it's necessary. Pain now. Pleasure later. And for some, even the pain, the process of getting stronger, becomes enjoyable. It is required.

ASK YOURSELF

- In what areas are you weak? Strong?
- Have you made plans to get strong in those weak areas? What are those plans?
- In what areas is your group weak? Strong?
- Have you all made plans to get strong in those weak areas? What are those plans?

CHALLENGE

Contemporary thinking says, "Ignore your weaknesses. Focus on your strengths." This implies that there is no need to be well balanced, but instead, very good at one or a few things. Consider both sides. Does this fit your situation? Does your job allow you to be really good in one area and terrible in all others? Does this theory play out in other areas of life? Consider and move forward.

I know it's uncomfortable,
but it's necessary.

PAiN >>
(Part 2)

When it comes to getting stronger, pain is expected. That's a fact. But you should be able to tell the difference between the pain associated with getting stronger and the unnecessary pain associated with operating incorrectly.

I used to work in a fitness center. During my last year there, this young lady came into my office crying. She begins to tell me about her recent exercise regime and shows me her swelling joints and muscles. Along with the swelling came a burning sensation and an unbearable amount of pain. She said it hurt to write, steer her car, get dressed and was fearful of other daily functions that soon could be affected. Since I wasn't a fitness professional, I gave her an over-the-counter response and encouraged her to seek a professional opinion. A few days later, she contacted me and let me know she was exercising incorrectly. Within a couple of weeks, she was back to exercising with a more suitable routine for her body.

Pain is expected, but there's a difference between good pain and bad pain.

When it comes to building group muscle, good pain comes from pushing the group into establishing new limits and developing new capabilities. This could look like clear and concise communication, following every level of protocol, monitoring input and feedback, and over-the-top professional transparency and accountability. Every exercise and movement within the group is intentionally done with an outcome in mind.

Bad pain comes from improper movement and abuse of the body/group. This could look like criticism without correction, one-way communication, gossip, back stabbing, non-delegation of responsibilities, blaming others, and not recognizing individual or group achievements.

One way builds the group. The other way tears it down. Both ways come with pain. It is up to the group to be able to discern between the two. If not, even the simplest tasks become labored and painful.

ASK YOURSELF

- Can you think of a time when you thought you were doing something good, but it was causing more harm than good?
- How did you repair your actions?
- Have you ever had to address someone who was doing the same thing?
- If so, how did the situation turn out? If not, why didn't you? What was the outcome?

CHALLENGE

We often judge ourselves based on our intentions and others on their actions. Let's make giant steps toward observing intentions and actions because considering both may lead to less unnecessary pain.

Be able to tell the difference between the pain associated with getting stronger and the unnecessary pain associated with operating incorrectly.

STOP GIVING PEOPLE "THE FINGER" >>

Nope. Not the finger you were thinking, although that one probably deserves a section all to itself, but not today. The finger I'm talking about is the pointer finger. That's right! The one people use when pointing at stuff, hence the name: pointer finger. The one used when identifying the object on which the pointer wants everyone else to focus. Most popularly used when referring to anything away from the individual of whom possesses the finger. What am I getting at? Stop giving people the finger!

You might say, "What if I'm giving directions? What if I'm applauding an effort? What if I'm identifying a thief? What if......?"

Oh hush! You know I'm not talking about that. I'm talking about the guy who never takes the blame. I'm talking about the girl that always shifts the focus away from herself. I'm talking about the boss who blames his direct reports. I'm talking about the person who, when crap hits the fan, he gives everyone around him—dun dun dun....THE FINGER!

Why? I'll give you three reasons.

1. You must work with these people after the boss leaves. Do you really want to operate in that kind of environment? No.
2. You burn bridges when you place the blame. People no longer feel like they can trust you.
3. You think it makes you look good or at least not as bad as the others. Guess what? It doesn't. Be a team player! A good gesture would be to absorb the hit as a team on the front side. And if it really wasn't your fault, address the individual on the back side.

There will be a time when identifying someone will be unavoidable. In these times, the person being singled out is dangerous to the group. But for the most part, we shouldn't be quick to place the blame or shift the focus. No scapegoats. Man up. Woman up. Be responsible. And if it isn't you, show grace and speak to the individual face to face instead of defaulting to the finger. There's no way a group will grow better together with a bunch of Judas Iscariots filling the room.

Stop giving people the finger!

ASK YOURSELF

- Have you ever been unjustly singled out? How did you feel?
- Have you ever been justly singled out? How did you feel?
- Has someone ever come to you face to face instead of revealing your error publicly or to someone up the chain of command? How did you feel?
- What is your personal, moral and ethical policy when identifying someone's error?

CHALLENGE

Treat others how you want to be treated. If you want the benefit of the doubt and opportunity to correct an error, provide others that same opportunity.

Show grace and speak to the individual face to face instead of defaulting to the finger.

E X P L O R E >>

Hello. My name is Derrick and I drive a 2003 Ford Explorer. It has 170,000 miles on it. I haven't had it long enough to name it, but I have definitely called it a few names in the past and none of those names have been used affectionately. I've had the timing chain, battery and fuel pump replaced, replaced all four tires and still have an estimated $1,200 of more work to put into it before I consider it to be in a good place. Did I mention I haven't had it a year yet? I won't even mention the work that was put into before I got it. Yet, with all of this in mind, every time I get into ol' Romo (one of my name options because it's blue and always lets me down), it starts up. And my hope is that the upfront cost will be a small investment for what I get out of the car later.

While at a coffee shop one morning, I overheard two guys talking. They used words like unreliable, undependable, quits on them without notice, etc. Their conversation was so negative, it sounded like they were talking about my car. It turns out they were talking about their group at work. I asked them, *why did they continue to work the job if the group was so bad?* Their reply was jumbled and took a while to settle on an answer. In short, they said that somehow, despite those characteristics, the group got stuff done. At the end of the day, week or project, regardless of how long it took them to get started or how many times they sputtered along the way or how unreliable others may have seemed during the process—at the end of the day, the group was able to deliver.

Listen, I have vented with the best of them. And by vented, I mean complained. (Let's remove the sugar from the poop.) But as I looked back over every group in which I've participated, my experience could have been exponentially more positive than what I made them out to be if I would have taken time to explore. And by explore, I mean discover the dynamics of your group! Look underneath, around and through the obvious. The surface shows sputter. Exploration sees the need for clarification or motivation. The surface shows lazy. Exploration sees someone who's burned out.

Don't get me wrong. Sometimes lazy is all there is to it. Sometimes a person sputters simply because they can't or won't grab a concept or responsibility. But I believe these occurrences are the exception and not the rule.

Take time to explore the dynamics within your group. While it may not ever run perfectly, this small and possibly tedious investment upfront will keep it going for a long time.

ASK YOURSELF

- What are some personal areas you sputter through in life?
- What are some professional areas you sputter though at work?
- Do your personal, social, and professional groups sputter?
- What are your plans to address those issues upfront to insure everything runs smoothly over time?

CHALLENGE

Don't ignore the warning signs and issues. Perform regular personal and professional maintenance. Invest on the front end.

FLOWERS >>

Let me start out by saying, I haven't always been a flower guy. I am now, but this is something that has happened recently. Here's the story:

I've known my officemate for seven years (and counting) and we've shared an office for five of those years. For four of those office years, not one plant cracked the threshold of our office. Suddenly, she starts dating someone who sends her flowers, not just regularly, but every Tuesday...for an entire year (and counting).

You read that right. Flowers. Every Tuesday. For a year....and counting.

During this time, I found myself growing soft on my all-but-certain stance against flowers. I've always thought flowers were a sweet gesture, but extremely generic and wasteful. But something happened when they were put in my office, in my space, in my face, time and time again. And all of a sudden, before I knew it, the phrase, "stop and smell the roses" began to resonate in my heart.

To me, "stop and smell the roses" means that flowers last for a season—a moment. They represent those precious seasons and moments in our lives that physically go away, but the scent remains. If we aren't careful, we'll rush past those moments. We will pass them up, expecting them to be there when we come back. We say to ourselves, "I'll have time for that later" and more than not, we never make it back to those flowers. And if we do, the moment has passed and it will never be the same as if we would have stopped, took a moment and smelled them when we initially saw them.

Take time to enjoy moments of success. Dance in the rain. Kiss in the park. Cry during a movie. Attend that reunion. Stay up late every now and again. Talk a minute longer. Exchange an extra text. Spend the extra dime. Say, "I love you" one more time than you think it necessary. Use your vacation instead of selling it back. Give a compliment. One extra high five. Hold that hug a second longer.

It's possible those moments may come back through again.

Then again, they may not.

ASK YOURSELF

- Can you think of a moment you wish you would have relished a little longer?
- Can you think of the reason you didn't cherish that moment?
- What did you gain for rushing past that moment?
- What did you lose for not having spent a little time at that moment?

CHALLENGE

Commit to cherishing a moment a little longer each day. It doesn't matter the size of the moment. Pull your spouse back in for an extra kiss. Run one more mile. Spend five more minutes with a friend. Or actually **stop** and smell some flowers. Whatever you do, just know that you're creating memories when you do it.

If we aren't careful, we'll rush past those moments. We will pass them up, expecting them to be there when we come back.

POPCORN >>

For my kids and me, the movies are kind of our thing. Nothing against mom, but the movies are almost a sacred experience between this dad and his kids. The entire process is also very ritualistic.

We talk about the movie from the time we leave home until the time we arrive at the theater. We talk about the movie from the car to the ticket window. After we leave the ticket window, we talk about the movie all the way to the—Now this is where it gets tricky. Normally, like,nine times out of 10, we get popcorn, a drink and candy, but it's really about the popcorn. Drinks are merely to wash down the salt and butter. Candy is for the sweet and salty combo. But it's really all about the popcorn. Every now and then, I pull the dad card just because I can, and we won't get popcorn. Those times immediately turn for the worse. My kids don't throw tantrums, but they are old enough to voice their displeasure. If they don't do it verbally, they do it through their demeanor. So, with or without popcorn, this is the way it plays out:

WITH POPCORN: Once we leave the ticket window, we talk about the movie all the way to the concession stand. We order snacks and they can choose popcorn with or without butter or salt, a beverage and candy. After paying and receiving the snacks, we talk about the movie from the concession stand to our seats. Previews roll. Popcorn is gone. Movie starts. I get them a refill so they don't miss the movie. I come back. They don't even eat half of the refill. Movie is great. Drink is gone. Candy makes its way out of the theater and into the backseat cushions of my car. Fun was had. Another movie experience in the books.

WITHOUT POPCORN: Once we leave the ticket window, we talk about the movie all the way to the—

"Wait. We aren't getting any popcorn?"

"Not today."

"Why not?"

"You guys ate before we left."

"But we always get popcorn."

"I know. We'll get it next time."

No more talking. Watch the movie. Go home. Mom asks, "How was the movie?"

The kids say, "Dad didn't get us any popcorn." Then they disperse throughout the house.

Like my kids, some people don't do well with sudden change. I'm sure this situation could have been better handled if I told them in advance that we wouldn't be getting popcorn this time or if I gave them a more in-depth explanation of why we weren't getting popcorn or if I would have gradually weaned them off popcorn entirely.

The same goes for these types of people in your group. Sudden change is unacceptable. They want to be involved at every level. If anything changes, they want to be on the front end of the decisions, involved with the decision-making process and part of the resolution.

Though ideal, the truth of the matter is including everyone in every step of the process isn't always going happen. Whether it has to do with poor planning or a sudden change of events, there are usually people in place to make those sudden decisions for the rest of the group. The responsibility of the group is to roll with the punches and be filled in later. This doesn't eliminate or replace accountability or communication. Hopefully, you're part of a company that will eventually inform everyone why the decision was made and how that resolution was reached. If you are not, you may want to attach yourself to an organization with more accountability and communication or become comfortable with not knowing. However, if you are a part of a company that has an effective flow of communication, just chill. It'll work out. Besides, in the grand scheme of things, when it comes down to it, it's just popcorn.

ASK YOURSELF

- Have you had a popcorn situation at your job? Explain.
- How are you with sudden and uncommunicated change?
- Does communication flow effectively within your group? Up and down the chain of command?
- If so, how can it improve? If not, how can effective communication be established?

CHALLENGE

When it comes to communication, don't be the weak link within the chain of command. Prepare enough in advance to communicate change. Adapt. Be clear. Specific. Open. Honest. Open to feedback. Ready to clean up messy situations.

Rolling with the punches doesn't eliminate or replace accountability or communication.

BUST A MOVE >>

I have a fitness friend who is always finding new ways to get me to be more active. Her solution: bust a move! Move often. Move for a sustained period of time. Have fun when you move. Move with other people. Move something heavy. Move in new ways. Just move. She makes it sound so easy. Just move, huh?

Detour.

I have another friend who has a truck. Anyone who owns a truck is likely to get all kinds of requests to move or haul something. He and his truck weren't any different. And whenever he got a call, he called me. I'd have to say, over 10 years, we've probably moved 20 homes together. The odd thing is that before then, I don't think we talked much outside a few social gatherings and moving people. Now, 20 moves later, he's one of my best friends. And it all began with moving.

Back on course.

If you want to have a healthy body, bust a move. Move often. Move for a sustained period of time. Have fun when you move. Move with other people. Move something heavy. Move in new ways.

If you want to have a healthy relationship with those around you, do the same. Bust a move, but with them. Bust a move together. Hang out often and for hours at a time. Have some stinkin' fun. Laugh loudly. Don't be afraid to talk about heavy things. Hang around other people together. Do new things with each other. Because if you do, your relationship with be healthier and stronger.

So, whether you want to get fit or better your relationships, bust a move.

ASK YOURSELF

- Who do you bust a move with?
- Why do you like busting a move with this person/those people?
- Can you imagine busting a move without them? If so, what does that look like?
- What does busting a move look like by yourself?

CHALLENGE

Move around! By yourself. With people. Bust new moves. Resurrect the old moves you used to bust. Just MOVE!

Don't be afraid to talk about heavy things.

RULES OF ENGAGEMENT >>

Before my wife and I got married, we went through few months of counseling. We thought it would be best to get some tools, sharpen a few skills and get some solid advice from a couple who had been through what we were getting ready to go through. During those few months counseling, we covered a lot of stuff. In fact, we've probably forgotten more than we remembered. However, there was one extremely important tool we walked away with that we still use today: rules of engagement.

Our rules of engagement are the guidelines by which we disagree. No matter how simple or complex the disagreement, we make sure to abide by these rules. Why? Because these rules help us to fight fair. No name-calling. No bringing up old, unrelated stuff. No leaving the property. No hitting. Use timeouts if things get too heated. We must finish the discussion before going to sleep or agree to continue at a later time.

You know, rules that create a healthy and safe environment in which people can disagree, be heard and maintain a positive relationship.

On the flip side, now that I know what healthy disagreement looks and feels like, it is painful to be a part of an unhealthy disagreement. I'm sure you can relate. It's difficult trying to resolve conflict with people who become defensive, point the finger, play the blame game, remain off-topic, interact emotionally, hold grudges, raise their voice, tense their posture, storm out of the room and are overly concerned with being right than maintaining the relationship.

I can't imagine what my marriage would be like if we had not established a few rules of engagement before getting married. Similarly, it would be unwise for any organization to not prepare for conflict. Conflict is inevitable. It is going to happen no matter how in-depth the hiring process or the number of people in the company. No matter the size or revenue of the company, conflict will arise. The best way to handle it is having rules (a plan) in place through which conflict can be resolved.

ASK YOURSELF

- Do you have personal rules of engagement?
- Do you belong to a group that has rules of engagement?
- Do those personal and group rules overlap? Where?
- Have you ever experienced a disagreement with someone who didn't have rules of engagement? What are some of the things you observed/ experienced?

CHALLENGE

Take the time to create rules of engagement. Whether they are personal or group, romantic or friendship, for church or sports team, make them! Create lines that you and others will not cross. Then make sure the people around you are aware of those lines. This will create a safe place of interaction and expectations for all sides.

Rules help us to fight fair.

THE WHITEBOARD >>

I would frequently visit a particular room at my old job. I would walk in and just sit. It was a conference room that had magnetic floor-to-ceiling whiteboards on all four walls. White tables were in the middle of the room surrounded by black desk chairs that leaned and swiveled. There was a projector mounted to the ceiling and pointed toward the front wall on which the computer station was placed in the corner. The lights could lighten or darken certain sections of the room. And to top it off, the room had conference call capabilities.

This room screamed creativity, hope, possibility, freshness, and exploration. The slightly worn carpet and smell of markers gave an extra witness to the seasoned use of the space. Every level of employee has walked through that door, sat in those chairs, wrote on those walls, clicked those buttons, spoke into those speakers and walked out better, stronger, more accomplished, enlightened and more energized than before they came in. (Or at least that's the hope.)

The whiteboard means writing, then erasing. It means getting rid of the good for something better. It means capturing a thought out of mid-air and putting on display for the world see. The whiteboard is where the pieces come together, where greatness is made, where the playing field of thought is equalized, where the writer becomes a servant to every mind around him. The whiteboard is for teams.

If you don't have one, you should. Put it in your office at work, in your house or wherever you spend the most time thinking, creating and planning. You should have one, not because it's a great visual tool for you and everyone else to see, but because it's an important piece of the imperfect creative process.

ASK YOURSELF

- Where do you keep your ideas?
- Who do you share your ideas with?
- What is your idea forming, brainstorming process?
- How often do you get into your creative space/ zone?

CHALLENGE

Get a whiteboard. Be creative. Explore often. Share it.

The whiteboard means writing, then erasing. It means getting rid of the good for something better. It means capturing a thought out of mid-air and putting on display for the world see.

SCiSSOR TEAMS >>
(Part 1)

My wife likes to do things together, only her and me. No one else. Like, side by side. I like to do things with her as well, but in a slightly different way. For example, if we are cooking dinner, she wants to work on the salad together. I'd rather her work on the salad and I work on another part of the meal or vice versa. If we are at the movies, she wants to stand in the line together, while I'd rather stand in line while she gets awesome seats. If we are watching the same show, she wants to watch it together, experiencing every scene at the exact same time. I, on the other hand, prefer to watch it whenever you can and the other person has to play catch up. Then, we'll talk about it later.

Over the years, I'm learning to think differently. Why? Because doing things my way puts more focus on the task and not the individual or experience. As my mother would say, "You can't focus so much on what you're cutting that you forget about the scissors." (She said this because I would focus so much on the paper that my fingers would get in the way of the scissors.)

My wife and I had grown so accustomed to doing things separately that working together had become an inconvenience, a nuisance and quite difficult. While she enjoyed dominating something together, I was always thinking of how much we could do separately. I felt locked down, tied together and restricted. I felt like my success and accomplishment was based on the production of someone else. While this approach possesses a bit of truth, there were some other things that could be accomplished only if we worked together.

Divide and conquer isn't always the best approach to getting things done. Sure, it is appropriate for many situations, but not every situation. Does every employee need to be at every meeting? No, but there should be at least a few meetings that every employee must attend. Should everyone work on the same project? No, but there are eventually going to be projects that everyone will be required to work on.

Working by yourself is a skill and, for many, a preference. But working with others is a commodity and takes time develop. Both are necessary and appropriate. The trick is not to be so concerned about the task that the people, group and experience are forgotten.

Don't focus so much on what you're cutting that you forget about the scissors.

ASK YOURSELF

- Do you prefer individual or group work?
- Do the people around you know your preference?
- How do you respond when required to work outside of your preference?
- Ask someone reliable the first three questions about you. Reflect on the response.

CHALLENGE

It's okay to have a preference. It is NOT okay to be unwilling to work outside of it. Become comfortable in both areas. This will expand your pool of people to work with and increase your tolerance for other workstyles.

Doing things my way puts more focus on the task and not the individual or experience.

SCiSSOR TEAMS >>
(Part 2)

The more I thought about my mother's scissor quote, the more I remembered that I used to think that scissors could be used for anything. Paper, chicken, rubber, clothes, wood, plants, wire—whatever I was trying to cut, scissors were my primary tool of choice. And my mother would get so mad! By the time she used the scissors for which she designated them, they were dull, dirty and ineffective. Hence her quote that I remember to this day, "You can't focus so much on what you're cutting that you forget about the scissors."

I notice that my kids were starting to do the same thing, but with many more other objects. Butter knives became flat-head screwdrivers. Screwdrivers became microphones. Pots and pans became drum sets. Buckets became step stools. And like me, scissors were being used for myriad of things I didn't even consider. So, I sat my kids down and explained to them how each object was meant to be used. After we covered all of the material, I asked them a few questions:

1.   What do you think the scissors were created to do?
2.   Could the scissors be damaged if you used them for something else?
3.   If you can't use the scissors, what tool do you need to complete the task?

The thing was, my kids were just trying to get the job done. They were using whatever they had to accomplish whatever they were trying to do.

When it comes to our groups and tasks, we can ask similar, if not the same, questions. Why did I hire this person? What is their skill set? Can I use them to complete a task outside of their skill set? Are they going to be effective in that setting? Where will they shine the most? Where will they have the most success? What task do I need accomplished? What type of person should I hire for that position? If we don't have the current personnel and can't hire anyone, who best meets the need? Can I combine people and skill sets to complete the task?

ASK YOURSELF

- What are some of your gift/talents/abilities that can be used in different areas?
- How often do you take the opportunity to use those abilities in different areas?
- Have you ever seen someone with an under-used gift/talent? Did you imagine what you would do with that particular ability?
- What are some abilities you are currently acquiring or developing? How do you plan to use those abilities?

CHALLENGE

For whatever reason, you're going to be tempted to withhold your gifts and talents from certain people or groups. I encourage you to use your abilities whenever possible. Your use of them will put you in places that you could never imagine. They will open doors, put you at tables, and get you in front of people, shaking hands and having conversations that you wouldn't have come across otherwise.

Use whatever you have to accomplish whatever needs to be done.

SCiSSOR TEAMS >>
(Part 3)

You know, there is something about this scissor concept that I just can't shake. The more I think about it, the more I absolutely love the concept of scissor teams. In part 1, we talked about how and why you should know how to work with another individual. In part 2, we talked about knowing your purpose and task you specifically can accomplish with your skillset. This time, we'll talk about scissors from the perspective of a dynamic duo: people feeding off each other, working in perfect harmony, sharpening each other, completing every task before them, both having equal participation. I love it.

There are different kinds of scissors that each cut and shape in a way that no other duo can. Look at Shaq and Kobe, Ben and Jerry, Batman and Robin, salt and pepper and Bert and Ernie, and Sonny and Cher.

Whether the relationship is food, music, business, or sports, they just work! Some work right off the back. Others work over time. They grow together to create this symbiotic relationship that leads right to success. And while this may not be the goal of every business encounter, everyone would be fortunate to come across at least one of these experiences in a lifetime.

Whatever it takes, find your scissor teammate.

ASK YOURSELF

- Who is your dynamic partner?
- Do you have more than one? Maybe in different areas?

- What do you love about having that partner?
- What does life/business look like without that partner?

CHALLENGE

If you don't have a go-to person, get one. Everyone needs one. It can be done alone, but it doesn't have to be. Growing is better when it's done together.

Some work right off the back.
Others work over time.

WRITE IT IN PEN >>

My brother and I have recently started writing letters to each other. While I enjoy the communication and nostalgia of getting written mail, what I enjoy the most is his penmanship. The bubble of his letters. The slant to his style. The digression of neat to sloppy as the letter gets longer. I can tell when he has taken a pause because of the vast difference in form from paragraph to paragraph. Sometimes he runs out of ink and has to change pens or color. When he gets on a roll, his words run closer together. When he makes mistakes, he scratches through them and keeps on going instead of starting a new sheet of paper.

I love it. Every single letter.

Ironically, he has lived his life the same way— in pen. Every mistake is obvious. Each smudge is apparent. It's easy to see when he's taken a break or changed direction because the writing is completely different when he begins again. Sometimes, when he changes the color or style of his life, I feel a bit thrown because the tone changes from that to which I've become accustomed. When he gets tired, his life begins to read a bit sloppy. He lives a better story when he's fresh. I like when he writes life with a certain style and color of pen compared to the others.

There's something to be said about a person who writes their life in pen. They are unashamed, transparent, colorful, open and blemished. Full of twists and turns. A beautiful story for all of the world to see, learn from and enjoy. These are the people with whom I want to live, work and play—them reading my story and I reading theirs'.

ASK YOURSELF

- What are some things you wished you would have lived in pencil?
- What are some things you're glad you lived in pen?
- How do you think those pen moments have shaped who you are?
- What are some things you hope to pen in your future? Personally? Professionally?

CHALLENGE

Everyone gets to write their own story. Choose and plan, then implement in pen a beautiful story for all of the world to read.

There's something to be said about a person who writes their life in pen.

JUST TAAAAAAAAP IT IN >>

When I first learned how to golf, I wanted to hit the ball hard and long. The next thing I wanted to do was learn how to shape my shots, which included moving the ball right, left, long with backspin or short with a forward bounce. Then I started to focus on my short game and now, putting.

I'm not sure how I would go about it if I had to do it all over again, but I do know that I would not have waited 15 years to start worrying about putting.

More times than I care to remember, there have been three people on the edge of the green waiting for me to complete my three or four putt melt-down. Their placating gestures of "unlucky" or "tough break" or "good line" or "good speed" are meant to encourage me, but often fuel the anger boiling beneath my skin. Yet, for some reason, once the round is done, I leave the course and don't even think about putting until it's time to play the next round. And then I tee it up, smash it down the fairway, throw one on the green in two and three putt for a bogey, and the anger resurfaces and the process repeats.

No matter how far I hit the ball or how well I shape the course, I'll never be the best golfer I can be until I learn how to putt. Why? Because success doesn't happen on the tee box, it happens on the green. Success doesn't happen in the air, it happens in the cup.

Comparably, greatness is in the ability to do the mundane consistently, in doing the small things well, in taking the small steps carefully, and in leaving no leaf unturned.

This is one of the hardest lessons I've ever learned. I wanted to be on stage, not write speeches. I wanted to speak from my heart, not script it out. I wanted to create on the fly instead of customize my approach. I wanted to drive the ball 300 yards, not tap it in a hole.

Now, as a fairly seasoned speaker, I've learned the value of writing. And as a mid-80s golfer, I've learned the value of putting. I stand over every ball and whisper to myself, "Just taaaap it in. Come on, Derrick. Just tap it in." I still miss a lot, but my focus is there.

Hopefully, as a manager, supervisor, team leader, husband, wife, parent, pastor, counselor, or car salesman, you've learned the value of listening, communicating, and motivating. These are the small things we tend to overlook, but end up being the most important.

So, in the midst of all of the great things happening in your group, don't forget to whisper to yourself every now and then, "Just taaaaap it in."

ASK YOURSELF

- What are some small things you need to get better at doing?
- How do you plan to get better in those areas?
- What are some small things in which your group(s) need to get better?
- How do those groups plan on getting better in those areas?

CHALLENGE

Find an area in your life that needs work. Focus on it. Dominate it. Find another area. Repeat.

Greatness is in the ability to do the mundane consistently.

JUST TASTE THE SOUP >>

A man goes to restaurant, gets a table and orders soup. The waiter sets the soup on the table and walks away. The man calls the waiter back to the table and says, "Taste the soup." The waiter replies, "Is the soup too hot or too cold?" The man replies, "Just taste the soup." The waiter replies, "Okay. Where's the spoon?" The man replies, while waving his finger at the waiter, "Aha!"

Just taste the soup— This is one of my most favorite lines in a joke. The joke was simple and rude, but definitely proved a point. The man could have easily asked the waiter for a spoon, but instead he added his own flare of sarcasm and humor to his request.

I've had to learn the hard way that everyone isn't going to share my sense of humor or appreciate my level of sarcasm. My parents get me. My kids get me. My wife, friends and business partners get me. However, I mustn't assume that everyone will get me—at least not right off the bat. There are so many variables at work when interpreting humor and sarcasm.

What is their experience with my kind of humor? How does my humor mix with their humor? Are they a literal type of person? Is this a high stress moment in which my sarcasm won't be appreciated? Have they had a hard/rough day? Am I joking about a topic that is sensitive to them? Do they just want/need a straight answer and I'm beating around the bush?

Sometimes, a simple joke or sarcastic remark can snowball into something offensive that breaches a relationship. I'm pretty sure that for most people, the last thing that's intended by their joke or sarcasm was to offend anyone, so we must be sure to gauge the moment and proceed appropriately.

Let's remember to stop and take a minute to think before saying things like *just taste the soup.*

ASK YOURSELF

- When was the last time you offended someone?
- Did you notice it or did they confront you about it?
- Were you able to clean up the moment?
- What is that relationship like now?

CHALLENGE

Become proficient at gauging people and situations. Observe the mood and moment, then respond accordingly. This is a rare talent needed in every group and social situation.

Sometimes, a simple joke or sarcastic remark can snowball into something offensive that breaches a relationship.

SPARK TO FIRE >>

Have you ever been a part of a group that moves from concept to completion quickly? One day you're brainstorming, and the next you're printing or placing an order for production. One day you're kidding about a topic, and the next day it's in the paper. One minute you're giggling, and the next minute it's full blown laughter and the inside story of the century. These are examples of when the "spark to fire" process is smooth and moves quickly.

It's true—This concept actually exists! Groups like this actually exist.

One minute, you're in your office crying and the next, you have the entire floor consoling you. An impromptu happy hour turns into a weekly ritual. A potluck turns into a smorgasbord. An idea turns into a company.

I've been part of a group like this and it's amazing. Unfortunately, this same group slowly turned into the exact opposite rather quickly. But in order to understand the transformation, you have to look at what prevents a group from moving from spark to fire.

Obstacles like insecurity, lack of communication, cliques, low commitment and poor work ethic prevent a group from moving from spark to fire. These things literally suck the air out of the group. They are the anti-fuel. They are fire suppressants. It is impossible to produce a spark in this environment. And where there is no spark, there is no fire.

People produce in environments in which they are confident in their abilities and secure in their position, communication and accountability run rampant, everyone is focused on the production and success of the group, which creates trust up, down and laterally within the chain of command. Everyone is allowed to be their truest selves. They are committed to the purpose and mission, comprehend direction and see the vision. Everyone works hard and they are rewarded in various ways for doing so.

Few things compare to the feeling of accomplishment. Above that, accomplishment with a sense of belonging and accountability. Above that, a vibe that makes you want to participate in that process again. Thus, the powerful appeal of moving from spark to fire.

ASK YOURSELF

- Think of a fire-to-spark experience you've had.
- Who/what was the spark?
- What did the fire look like at the end?
- Do you think that process can be replicated with different people, different settings and different goals?

CHALLENGE

Be the spark! Be the fuel! Contribute to the fire! Whatever you do, just don't be the suppressant. (See "Party Pooper.")

Obstacles like insecurity, lack of communication, cliques, low commitment and poor work ethic prevent a group from moving from spark to fire.

MORALITY AT WORK >>

Before we get started, I want to acknowledge that this section may be a stretch for some. Especially those who work in hard sciences, law or privacy based services. For those professions, ethics serve as the nervous system for their body of work. Without an ethical standard, things get muddy and lines begin to blur. But hear me out.

As a teenager, I worked at summer camps and afterschool programs. It was pretty sweet. I worked with peers, managed younger people, played all day, ate free lunch, built relationships that remain to this day and even got to make quite a bit of money. To say the least, it was the experience of a lifetime. We stayed in trouble, but had a lot of fun too. I'm sure if I polled the rest of the staff that their experience would be pretty similar. Well, all except for one—Stacy.

Stacy was by the book and the reason the camp staff stayed in so much trouble. Needless to say, she didn't mesh well with the rest of the teenage staff. Of course, being a staff of teenagers, we made our fair share of mistakes. And the truth be told, we did break the rules, so we can't completely shove Stacy under the bus for telling on us. Stacy saw everything as right or wrong and would report everything, in detail, back to the camp director, instead of handling it one on one.

Fast forward to adult life when I worked with a man named Don. He was very much like Stacy and saw things as black and white, right or wrong. He did his job and expected everyone else to do theirs. He knew the chain of command and stuck to it. He didn't offer a courtesy correction, didn't socialize outside of work, clocked in on time and didn't stay late, methodically completed every task and worked to the beat of his job description drum. As a result of this approach to his job, he gained a reputation for being coarse, short, abrasive, distant, a poor team player and unreceptive. Because I knew of his growing reputation and considered him a friend, I tried to approach him unofficially and off the record. And to my surprise, he was still coarse, short, abrasive, distant and unreceptive. In fact, his reply was, "If you have a problem with me, talk to my supervisor." Keep in mind, not only were we coworkers, I considered this guy a friend. And that was still his reply.

Short recap: Stacy went to the camp director. I chose to go to Don.

There are a few ways to look at these situations. If you say nothing, that means standing by and watching your coworker break the rules. I wouldn't necessarily recommend this option. Someone could get fired, the company could be misrepresented, someone could get hurt, productivity could decrease, and eventually everyone could be affected.

If you do what Stacy did and not talk to the people making the bad decision and go directly to the camp director, you may isolate yourself from the group, be known as someone who doesn't play well with others, create more work for your supervisor in the way of disciplinary actions/firing/hiring and decrease job specific productivity. But the situation is still being addressed. If you do what I did and say something to Don, you risk rejection or the possibility of that person being receptive and open to change.

In every single case, I choose the last one. Why? While ethics run the office, morality runs the world. I believe most people would appreciate the casual courtesy of being approached first before taking official actions against their behavior. And before you jump to the legal implications of not telling, I don't believe the majority of grey actions carry a significant reprehensible consequence. And those that do are not the aim of this section. By all means, if someone is abusive, harmfully neglectful, stealing, leaking information—what else?—feeding nuclear codes….then it is your ethical and contractual obligation to report those actions. But these are rare.

More immediately applicable and identifiable are those actions that toe the ethical line, but in more detail, reveal the morality of someone in their professional setting. In those cases, many of those things can be addressed at a coworker level. If that person is not receptive and continues, then upper management should be notified. Just my two cents.

Whatever you choose, I think there are several things to consider:

1. Is there a procedure already put in place? What is it? Does is apply?
2. How would you like to be treated?
3. Know who you are working with and how they expect to be treated as well.

Often times, ethics feel cold, whereas morals feel warm, closer to home and closer to the heart. Hopefully, you are doing what you love with people you enjoy. When you do what you love with people you enjoy, it feels less like work and more personal. When you work with people you enjoy, you want to see them succeed, even if that means giving them second chances. This is where grace or morality covers the iron hand of ethics. Not replacing one with the other, but instead creating an ebb and flow of both.

ASK YOURSELF

- Have you worked with a Stacy before? How did the group treat her?
- Have you worked with a Don before? How did the group treat him?
- Which do you believe to be the best option? Why?
- Have you ever had to make one of these decisions regarding a coworker? How did that situation turn out?

CHALLENGE

Be a giver of second chances. Extend the grace you aim to receive. Don't color every picture with black and white crayons.

While ethics run the office, morality runs the world.

L i K E M i K E >>

Growing up in the late 80s and early 90s, everyone wanted to be like Michael Jordan. People stuck out their tongues like Mike. People wore his shoes. People wore his jersey. They even showed up in record numbers for his movie. Mike was in music videos. He was on cereal boxes. Mike was the man.

But I never wanted to be like Mike. I wanted to be like Scottie Pippen. Scottie was the glue of the team. He was the sticky stuff between Mike and the rest of the team. He did all of the dirty work. When Mike was yinging, Scottie was yanging. When Mike left, Scottie stayed. While Mike was doing interviews and photoshoots, Scottie was warming up and cooling down. When Mike was tending to the media, Scottie was tending to the team. Nothing against Mike. I just wanted to be like Scottie.

I understood what people were saying when they said they wanted to be like Mike. Being like Mike was equated to be the best. There is nothing wrong with being the best. It pushes you to try your hardest. It's a benchmark for success and achievement. Being like Mike was like saying, "I want to do better than everyone else in the world." That's not a bad goal to have. But I think people would tend to take it a bit too far.

I've heard, "If I don't place first, I don't want to place at all."

ME: I'd gladly take a second or third place medal. And so would everyone else who didn't place.

I've heard, "Second place is the first loser."

ME: I always thought second place was far from the worst, although not the best.

I've heard, "Don't play second fiddle to anyone."

ME: Well, if I don't play it, someone else will, on stage, next to the first fiddle.

This perspective isn't one of laziness or an excuse for sucking. I get it. Some people use this as a means as to justify their losing. However, I refuse to shame my effort, especially if it was genuine. Scottie has just as many rings as Jordan. He rode on the same bus, played in the same arenas, dribbled and shot the same ball, squeaked the same court with his shoes, laced up in the same locker room, cleaned up in the same showers, and was coached by the same genius. I'm talking about Scottie **AND** Mike.

If I say so myself, being like Mike would be pretty awesome. But being like Scottie puts you at the same table.

ASK YOURSELF

- Who have you compared yourself to in the past? Why?
- Do you still compare yourself to that person? Why or why not?
- Have you ever tried a combination of people? Maybe the best attributes of many instead of the entire person of one?
- Do you think comparison is healthy for the comparer? Why or why not?

CHALLENGE

Be the best version of yourself. Not the best imitation of someone else.

I refuse to shame my effort, especially if it was genuine.

BUT DiD i GET AN A? >>

I spent a spring semester adjunct teaching for my alma mater. It was quite the experience. I was not only able to teach in the same classrooms in which I was taught, but also teach alongside the professors who taught me. I did not consider myself an equal, but privileged to be a part of the educational process. Hands down, one of the most exciting five months of my life.

Leading up to the semester, I searched for textbooks, created my schedule and established my lesson plans. I also did some research on the students who would be in my class. What were their tendencies? Who missed classes? Who were my hard workers, know-it-alls, athletes and seniors? Needless to say, I wanted to be prepared.

On the first day of class, I stepped into the classroom, inhaled a big breath of collegiate air and exhaled two lungs full of excitement. I was ready to go. After scanning the group of 10 students, confirming their information, previewing the semester for them and taking questions, I overheard one of the students mumble to the side, "Man, I just need an A in this class." From that moment until the end of the semester, that was her stance for every assignment, test and quiz. She knew exactly how many classes she could miss to get all of her attendance points. Her site visits and experiential tutorials were always followed up with, "Did I get an A?"

Her final was pretty sweet. She was tasked to create a game, activity or sport that had not been invented before. This required a fair amount of research and creativity. She did great! Her presentation was in-depth and her concept should have been patented. As I was trying to tell her all of these things, she nodded as to hurry me along, but eventually interrupted with, "But did I get an A?" I crunched the numbers, which included her final, and she did, in fact, get an A.

As a teacher, I wanted her to focus on the process, but she was focused on the outcome.

There are going to be outcome-oriented people in every group. Some may stomp over people, bend/break rules, cut corners, sever relationships, chameleon their personality, cheat the system and belittle leadership, while others may just miss the character building moments, devalue the process, do damage control along the way and ignore teachable moments. Whichever the case, some people just want to get to the end, achieve their goal and say they finished. To them, completion and production are the most important things.

I would say that finishing is important, but just as important is what you learn during the process. If you're going to be a part of the group, learn about your group mates and what you all are working together to accomplish. If you're going to take a class, actually learn something while you're there. Because if you don't, you will get an A, but won't learn anything in the process.

"A mode" = ignoring and devaluing the process just to get what you want at the end.

ASK YOURSELF

- When was the last time you were in "A mode?"
- Looking back, would you have done it differently? Why or why not?
- Do you think it's easy to be in "A mode" with people?
- Has someone ever been in "A mode" with you? If so, how did it make you feel?

Learn first. Understand second. Everything else significant will follow.

If you aren't careful, you'll get an A, but won't learn anything.

i'LL TAKE SECONDS >>

Typically, people ask for more of the things they don't need. "You know, I probably shouldn't, but I'll take another [insert food/drink/episode]." Recently, I've found a group of fitness people who pride themselves on asking for seconds of punishment... I mean, exercise. It's amazing actually. They'll complete the number of repetitions they set out to reach and then they'll do some more. I used to think that I didn't possess whatever that thing is that makes you want to do more, but I've isolated it to just exercise. When it comes to exercise, I complete my task and move on. But when it comes to other things, it clicks.

I can be reading a book and say, "One more chapter." I can look at my schedule and say, "I can squeeze in one more meeting." When hanging with friends, I look at the clock and say, "Okay, fifteen more minutes." When I'm playing with my son, I'll agree to one more game. My wife hesitantly allows me just one more kiss. When I'm following up with clients, one more call. When I'm writing, one more paragraph. When I'm researching, one more study. When I'm grading, one more paper. And before I know it, I've completed what I set out to complete, plus some!

Take a mental note of the hungry people in your group. Not food, silly. I'm talking about their drive and ambition. Are they jockeying for position or do they pursue team success? Do they try to monopolize the boss' attention or is the amount of time they spend together organic? Do they acquire knowledge for arrogance or for growth? Do they share resources with others or gobble it all up for the sake of exclusivity? Are they productive when they stay late or milking the clock for pay and appearance?

Sometimes, more is good. Sometimes, more is bad. I think it has more to do with the content than the amount, the intent more than the perception. Admittedly, I cringe as I'm writing this because I'm a more type of guy. I've prided myself on being able to do a lot, to always be able to handle seconds. But it's good because I'm preaching to myself. More isn't always better. I encourage you to remind yourself as well. Maybe you shouldn't get seconds this time. Maybe more isn't better. And when it comes to others, keep an eye for who's going back for seconds.

ASK YOURSELF

- What are some good things for which you ask seconds?
- What are some bad things for which you ask or seconds?
- How do these things help or hurt you?
- Are you able to recognize this in others around you? How does that affect your relationship with them?

CHALLENGE

Learn when and how to ask for seconds.

More isn't always better.

SHE FITS, BUT DOES SHE BELONG? >>

Remember the Lego project I completed with my son earlier in this book? It took us two hours to complete and even then, there were some things that could have been added. As a result of trying to quickly bring this activity to completion, I lost focus and started placing things in the wrong place.

Immediately, my son stopped working on his side of the project and began taking the incorrect pieces off the board from my side. I said, "Hey man, I just put those there." He firmly replied, "Just because the holes fit, doesn't mean you should put them there."

For the first two hours of his project, I was able to contribute effectively. He didn't object to my addition or placement until I began to do it incorrectly. And he was right, the princess didn't belong in the stable. She belonged in the tower so the prince could rescue her. I was all out of place. I lost focus. I forgot the point of this entire project. What we had built could potentially be ruined by the misplacement of one piece.

The same with any project or group within an organization. Just because someone has the credentials, doesn't mean they are the right fit. Just because it was the first or only suggestion, doesn't mean it's the best or right solution for the project. And if the leaders of the organization or manager of the project loses focus, the vision will be lost, goals will not be met and full potential will not be reached.

So, before you put the princess in the stable, ask yourself: I know she fits, but is that where she belongs?

- Have you ever been in a position where you didn't fit? How did you perform? Did you enjoy your time there?
- Have you ever worked with someone who was in a position in which they didn't belong? How did they perform? How did everyone else respond that person?
- How do misplaced people affect the efficiency of the group?
- How do misplaced people affect the morale of the group?

CHALLENGE

Make sure you fit. Do you line up with the people around you? In your thoughts and actions? Is your company, church, family, relationships, and/or community headed in the direction you want to go?

Just because someone has the credentials, doesn't mean they are the right fit.

WHAT DOES HE DO? >>

Accountability should be a key component of every work environment. Everyone should answer to someone. Someone should be aware of what you are doing, how you are doing it, when and where you are doing it, and why you are doing it. The more abstract and secluded someone becomes, the more likely they are to go rogue.

There was a guy named Sam at my old job who made the company a bunch of money. And because of this one feat, he received a large portion of autonomy. He reported directly to the VP of his department. He often came to work late and left early. He took long lunches. He drove a company vehicle, carried a company phone, used a company laptop, received weekly stipends on top of his salary, as well as received bi-annual bonuses and raises. Now, this may seem fairly normal for some individuals, but the thing was that only a few people knew what he did.

The more people began to notice the perks and low accountability, the more people started to ask questions. And when people started asking questions and were not getting sufficient answers, the entire lower two-thirds of the department began to grumble. WHY? The majority were in the dark. There was low communication. Information was secluded from large portions of the group. Direction was minimal. Instruction was nearly non-existent. And it appeared to be favoritism.

As a result of this festering environment, people began to mirror some of the same behavior Sam displayed, but without the permission. This caused the department to eventually have an emergency meeting to correct the growing negative behavior and address the foggy areas created by ambiguous explanations and what appeared to be preferential treatment.

After the meeting, everyone became clear of who Sam was and what he did. Many of them disagreed with the preferential treatment, but at least everyone knew what and why. They were also directed in the ways in which they were expected to behave and operate at work, even though they were admittedly different to Sam's position.

Finally, everything became clear. The department regained its focus. Communication took place. Accountability (laterally, ascending and descending) was restored. Operations not only smoothed out, but also increased in production and cohesion. Everything wasn't perfect, but expectations were clear.

Accountability must be a key component to every work environment. If communication remains clear, constant and consistent, everyone stays on board and the train keeps moving forward. In this case, it had to do with job descriptions and expectations, but that may not be YOUR situation. You could be dealing with vision and direction of the company. You could be dealing with promotion and raises, conflict resolution, healthy communication, delegation and/or strategic planning. The questions could easily turn from, "What does he do?" to "What do I do?" or "What am I doing?" or "What are we doing?" or "Where are we going?" Whatever the question or situation, accountability through action and communication is necessary for every person, group and company.

ASK YOURSELF

- Are you clear about your position and function within your group/organization?
- Is everyone around you clear about your position and function within your group/organization?

- Do you know the mission, vision, philosophy and direction of your organization?
- What does low accountability look like to you? High accountability?

CHALLENGE

Pursue accountability by asking questions and being transparent.

Accountability is a key component to the health of every social environment.

WHO'S NOT PLAYING? >>

I remember the day I decided I was going to pretend to play my clarinet in middle school band. I wasn't the best, but I also wasn't the worst—always a solid and consistent three through five chair. So, in a band of 35 instruments, I thought, "Who would miss a measly clarinet, right?" My teacher Mr. Curtis' stick went high into the air and when it came down, everyone began to play, but me. A few measures in, I could see his face began to sour up and his head began to tilt towards the clarinet section. There was no way he knew that I wasn't playing.

Eventually, overcome with frustration, after starting and stopping a few times, he singles out every single clarinet and makes them play by themselves. Along the way, he gave note, fingering, tempo and dynamics instruction to every single person. After the impromptu solos, he raised his hands in the air, dropped them and again, everyone began to play, but me. A few measures in, he steps down from the podium, continued to direct, but walked around the clarinet section with his ear tilted toward the bell of the instruments.

Of course, when he came by me, I began to play and when he walked away, I stopped. Eventually, he stopped the music again, placed his stick on the podium, both hands on his hips and asked, "Who is it?" Everyone in the clarinet section looked toward me. It took me three weeks to make it back to my spot of middle chair and another two weeks to make it to second chair. After that, I never got any higher. (Tiffany, the number one chair, was super good!)

There's always going to be that one guy who claims he wants to play, but he won't put forth the effort. Or he'll put forth the effort to get the position, but relaxes once he gets it. He won't continue to grow. He'll do just enough to not be the worst, but won't do more to be the best. It may look like everything is good, but everyone knows that he isn't pulling his weight. Even if the boss doesn't know, everyone close to him knows. Additionally, no one can complete their task because he is holding back the team where they can't ever finish or reach their full potential. The team will never be complete until everyone plays their part.

Our job as a direct report, coworker or superior is to shed light on this situation for the sake of the team. We must rise above the fear of conflict and above the hope that it will work itself out. If the situation is addressed, it moves closer to being resolved. And once addressed (as my conductor did by moving me to the last chair in my section), if not fired, that person has the option to sulk and settle for less or work hard and prove he deserves to be a part of the team. Because just like in music, every note is needed, every instrument counts and everyone is expected to play their part.

ASK YOURSELF

- What makes people choose to not play their part?
- How does that decision impact the rest of the team?
- How should that person be addressed?
- What happens to the individual and group when that person isn't addressed?

CHALLENGE

Play your part every single day. Play hard. Play fair. Play with others in mind. Show up. Contribute. Every single day.

The team will never be complete until everyone plays their part.

DO YOU TRUST ME? >>

Hands down, this is one of my favorite lines from Aladdin. It's said during the scene where a poor boy from the city and a princess get caught in the middle of trouble. In the process of saving her, the poor boy stretches out his hand to bring her to safety. Of course, she is hesitant. To ease her concerns, with his hand extended, he asks, "Do you trust me?" Later in the movie, this same boy has found a lamp with a genie inside. One of his wishes is to become a prince so he could win the heart of the princess he met in the city. While trying to woo her, he invites on a magic carpet ride. She's hesitant to get on the carpet as she's never rode one before. In order to ease her nerves, he stretches out his hand and asks her again, "Do you trust me?" This immediately lets her know that the poor city boy and the prince are the same person.

If you are genuine, it won't matter if you are the head or the tail, at the top or the bottom, the first or the last; you will be identifiable by your character. Whatever you were at the bottom will be magnified by your success.

There are some people who say that success changes people. I would reply that the change you see in people is the core of who those people were anyway. The core of who you are should be a constant. When things get rough and tough, your core should anchor your character. Your core grounds the soul and keeps the heart true to north. When this happens, your position or status won't shape who you are. Instead, it will allow you to be more of who you are. When this happens, you'll be able to reach out your hand to the world and to the people around you...and they will trust you.

ASK YOURSELF

- Do you know people who have appeared to change with success? Was the change positive or negative?
- How did people respond to that change?
- Do you know people whose character has been magnified by their success?
- Have you caught yourself changing in relation to success? How did you handle it?

CHALLENGE

Determine who you are now, before success arrives.

Whatever you were at the bottom will be magnified by your success.

EPILOGUE >>

Being a team player isn't a contemporary construct. Noticing the people and the world around us isn't a unique skill. It's not a gift. It's not a talent. Everyone is born with the innate ability to do so. Anyone with a willing heart has access to it. If the soul is open and the ears desire to hear, then acknowledging others and interacting intimately with our surroundings will happen naturally.

However, often times we choose not to go against what is designed to be a natural part of human existence. We choose not to participate in a deeper level of interaction with the world around us because of the amount of effort that is required. For whatever reason, we become afraid of the interaction, selfish with our time, gifts and talents. We sparingly sow into others our passion and love. And I get it. It's easier to live life thinking about ourselves. It is safe and comfortable. It is predictable. You don't have to consider the variables that accompany other people. Considering others definitely requires more effort. But it limits the depth and fullness at which life can be experienced.

Each individual brings their preferences, biases, world view, hygiene, morals, experiences, appetites, traditions, passions and everything else that makes them uniquely them. And getting all of these folks on the same page is hard. But community and inclusiveness leads to building something infinite and lasting; something stronger and diverse. That is the purpose of community. That is the reward of selflessness.

John F. Kennedy once said, "Ask not what your country can do for you, ask what you can do for your country."

When we are consumed by our own wants and drowned in our own perception, we lose the bigger picture of life. In fact, I would say the inward look only exists to discover where we fit in the world around us. Think about it. If I only chose have to do things based on how I felt or how I saw it, anyone who interacted with me would have to feel and see life the exact same way that I do. This shrinks my world down to...well, about one person. Me. That is not the essence of community.

The essence of community speaks to how we exist with others. Can our individual ability complement each other? (Yin & Yang) I can work in this group, but is it the right fit? (She Fits, but Does She Belong?) How can I be a better teammate? (Like Mike) How can I take responsibility of my own actions instead of blaming others? (Stop Giving People the Finger) These are all questions we have to ask ourselves when deciding where and how we belong. Not only do we ask ourselves, but we have the privilege and responsibility to ask others, making sure they fit and fulfill their purpose.

It's bigger than any one person. It's bigger than my feelings. It's bigger than your feelings. It's about the group. It's about the community. How can we all succeed together? How can we all move forward as one? How can we all grow stronger, get better at whatever we are interested in and how can we do all of that together? The answer is closer than you think. In fact, the answer is all around you. Every single day, you have the opportunity to grow better together. Schedule moments to have fun. Don't be afraid to redirect each other. Dance. Laugh. Work hard. Be creative. Celebrate individual accomplishments and group efforts. Serve one another. Reach up, out and down to build personal and professional relationships on all levels. Step outside of your comfort zone. Reach into areas you once considered inconvenient. Build relationships that challenge you. There are opportunities to grow better together all around you, every single day.

Even more importantly, the individual doesn't have to be sacrificed for the sake of the group. This is one of the fears of group thinking and team play. It used to be one of my personal fears. This fear actually prevented me from participating and contributing to anything significant for several years. I wasted years of my life because I didn't want to conform or be a part of a group effort. I was held hostage by what I considered to be individuality. Will my individuality be lost? Will I be heard? What about my feelings, ideas, preferences, unique perspective and individual career path? I froze and, in turn, did nothing. I was seen as selfish and a poor teammate who hoarded his gifts and talents and feared commitment. If you are reading this book and you think like the old me, please step out of this box. Step out and run far away. No one reaches their full potential by themselves. The best in you will be polished and shined by rubbing against others with gifts and talents. You can only be shaped by the appropriate tools of others.

Additionally, a good, solid, functional and forward thinking group considers the individual while operating as a team. There will be plenty of opportunity for the individual to be acknowledged and celebrated. There will be smaller projects that must be led with the collective goal in mind. Pieces must be individually placed in order for something great to be built. In most settings, there are leaders of five, 10, 20 and 50 people. Ultimately, there will be those who have no desire to be seen. But for others, for you, there will be opportunities to stand out amongst the group. Work hard. Be honest and sincere. Think of others. Build relationships. Be passionate. And your individual effort will benefit the group you're in.

Finally, being a strong individual within a group is one of the greatest things you will ever learn to do. Why? You will not be thinking only about yourself and you will not be thinking only about the group. It's not one way or the other. It's both. It's existing as an individual link on a chain. It's playing your position on the court. It's holding the hand of the person on both sides of you in the middle of an intense game of Red Rover. It's rubbing your iron against another's so you both can remain sharp.

It's being flexible and rigid. It's being a spark in the fire. It's learning how to think WE when every part of you is pulling for I. It's the epitome of being a team player.

Only the greats acknowledge and pursue this concept. Hopefully, since you have reached the end of this book, you will adopt this line of thinking and join the great people who are strong enough to stand out as a team player.

Here's one last challenge. Find out how you can individually make your team better. Make it a personal goal. Invest in your group for the sake of an overall improvement. I promise, the work environment will get better, and you will individually benefit as well.

A beautiful yard is made of beautiful blades of grass. The same for bricks on a building, drops in the ocean, petals of a rose, the voice in a chorus, the note within a harmony; each piece playing its collective part, yet possessing the ability to beautifully stand alone.

Made in the USA
Middletown, DE
21 March 2017